Sukiyaki(Kansai style)
すき焼き(関西風)

➡P134

Grilled Fish
焼き魚

➡P86

Somen Noodles
そうめん

Photo：まるうさん/写真AC

➡P060

Side Dishes
副菜

➡P102

Japanese Sweets
和菓子

➡P158,170

Character Bento

キャラ弁

➡P179

Boy's Day
こどもの日

Photo : Shinya nakamura/shutterstock

Girl's Day
ひな祭り

Photo : ziggy_mars/shutterstock

➡P186

Kaiseki

会席

➡P101

はじめに　Message to the Readers

　海外での和食への関心は高まる一方です。今や「和食＝鮨」のイメージをはる
かに超えて、ラーメンから吟醸酒、ひいては日本の発酵技術も注目され、世界の
トップシェフが麹を活用するほどになっています。筆者自身、アメリカ在住の食
のジャーナリストとして、また和食文化を紹介するラジオ番組の司会・プロデュー
サーとして、和食に魅了された外国人の話を聞く機会が多く、日本人としてとて
も誇らしく感じます。

　同時に、和食の素晴らしさを正確に伝えるのはなんと難しいことでしょう！
知っているはずが実は知らなかったり、文化的背景を説明しきれなかったり。そ
んなもどかしい思いを、少しでもなくすことができたらという思いから生まれた
のが本書です。

　第1章では和食の礎である価値観を紹介。第2章は代表的な料理、第3章は飲
み物、第4章は和菓子、第5章は弁当、行事食、洋食を、第6章では地方料理を
説明します。通訳案内の助けとして、気軽に英語を学ぶテキストとして、あるい
は和食のうんちくガイドとして、自由に活用できる内容になっています。

　これから和食は世界に広がりながら、ますます豊かに発展してゆくでしょう。
この本を読んで下さる方が、そんなプロセスに楽しく加わっていかれますように。

　Japanese cuisine (*washoku*) is unique, delicious and healthy. Sushi, ramen,
matcha, kaiseki … there is so much to discover. However, for many
foreigners, Japanese cuisine seems somewhat mysterious and elusive, partly
because of the language and cultural barriers.
　This book is Japanese cuisine 101. As you can see, it is primarily designed
for a Japanese audience who want to introduce *washoku* to foreigners in
English. But the book also covers all the essential elements of *washoku* from
philosophical backgrounds, regional characteristics to why you should slurp
when eating a bowl of ramen.
　Bring this with you on your trip to Japan, or to your local Japanese
restaurant. You will have a way more enjoyable and delicious experience
with *washoku*.

　Bon Appétit / *Itadakimasu!*

Akiko Katayama

目次

はじめに ──────── 1 　　本書の使い方 ──────── 4

1章 和食の基本
The Basics of *Washoku*

和食とは？ ──────── 6
自然の恵みと季節性 ──────── 8
敬意と感謝 ──────── 10
日本風のおもてなし ──────── 12
一汁三菜 ──────── 14

五味五色五法 ──────── 16
栄養豊富な和食 ──────── 18
出汁 ──────── 20
調味料 ──────── 22

2章 定番の和食
Popular Dishes of *Washoku*

主食① 米 Rice ──────── 28
01 ご飯の炊き方 How to Cook Rice ──────── 30
02 ご飯もの *Gohan Mono* ──────── 32
03 ご飯もの *Gohan Mono* ──────── 34
04 お茶漬け・雑炊 *Ochazuke/Zosui* ──────── 36
05 親子丼 *Oyako Don* ──────── 38
06 天丼 *Tendon* ──────── 40
07 鮨 *Sushi* ──────── 42
08 餅 Rice Cake ──────── 44
09 カレーライス Japanese Curry ──────── 46
主食② 日本の麺料理 Japanese Noodles ── 48
10 ラーメン *Ramen* ──────── 50
11 様々なラーメン Various *Ramen* ──────── 52
12 焼きそば *Yakisoba* ──────── 54
13 そば *Soba* ──────── 56
14 うどん *Udon* ──────── 58
15 そうめん *Somen* ──────── 60
主食③ 日本のパン Japanese Bread ──────── 62
16 菓子パン Sweet Pastries ──────── 64
17 惣菜パン Savory Breads ──────── 66
主菜① 日本の肉料理 Japanese Meat Dishes - 68
18 唐揚げ *Karaage* ──────── 70
19 トンカツ *Tonkatsu* ──────── 72
20 生姜焼き *Shoga Yaki* ──────── 74
21 照り焼き *Teriyaki* ──────── 76
22 焼き鳥 *Yakitori* ──────── 78
23 角煮 Braised Pork Belly ──────── 80
24 もつ料理 Organ Meats ──────── 82
主菜② 日本の魚料理 Japanese Fish Dishes ── 84
25 焼き魚 Grilled Fish ──────── 86

26 煮付け Simmered Fish ──────── 88
27 南蛮漬け *Nanbanzuke* ──────── 90
28 天ぷら *Tempura* ──────── 92
29 うなぎ丼 *Unagi Don* ──────── 94
30 刺身 *Sashimi* ──────── 96
31 刺身の魚 Fish For *Sashimi* ──────── 98
32 コラム：魚の珍しい部分 ──────── 100
33 コラム：会席 ──────── 101
副菜 Side dishes ──────── 102
34 たまご料理 Egg Dishes ──────── 104
35 納豆 *Natto* ──────── 106
36 豆腐 *Tofu* ──────── 108
37 肉じゃが *Nikujaga* ──────── 110
38 煮物 Simmered Dish ──────── 112
39 酢の物 *Sunomono* ──────── 114
40 和え物 *Aemono* ──────── 116
41 田楽 *Dengaku* ──────── 118
42 コラム：のり ──────── 120
43 コラム：漬物 ──────── 121
汁物 Soups ──────── 122
44 味噌汁 *Miso* Soup ──────── 124
45 吸い物 *Suimono* ──────── 126
鍋料理 Hot Pot ──────── 128
46 寄せ鍋 *Yosenabe* ──────── 130
47 おでん *Oden* ──────── 132
48 すきやき *Sukiyaki* ──────── 134
49 しゃぶしゃぶ *Shabu Shabu* ──────── 136
50 湯豆腐 *Yudofu* ──────── 138
51 コラム：居酒屋文化 ──────── 140

CONTENTS

3章 飲み物
Bevarages

飲み物① 日本茶 Japanese Tea ——— 142
52 日本茶 Japanese Tea ——— 144
53 抹茶 Matcha ——— 146
飲み物② 日本のアルコール
　　　 Alcohol Beverages of Japan ——— 148

54 日本酒 Sake ——— 150
55 焼酎 Shochu ——— 152
56 その他 Other Types of Alcohol ——— 154
57 コラム：カクテル文化 ——— 156

4章 和菓子
Japanese Sweets

和菓子 Japanese Sweets ——— 158
58 餅菓子 Mochi Sweets ——— 160
59 団子 Dango ——— 162
60 饅頭 Manju ——— 164

61 鯛焼きとどら焼き Taiyaki & Dorayaki ——— 166
62 クラッカーとキャンデ Crackers & Candy ——— 168
63 コラム：和菓子と茶道 ——— 170

5章 様々な和食のスタイル
Various Styles of *Washoku*

日本の弁当文化 Japanese Bento Culture ——— 172
64 幕の内弁当 Makunouchi Bento ——— 174
65-67 駅弁 Ekiben ——— 176
68 コラム：弁当箱のデザイン ——— 178
69 コラム：キャラ弁 ——— 179
行事食 Festive Fare ——— 180
70 年越しそば Toshikoshi Soba ——— 182

71 新年のご馳走 New Year Feast ——— 184
72 子供のための祝いの食べ物 Children's Fare ——— 186
洋食 Yoshoku ——— 188
73 オムライス Omu rice ——— 190
74 ハンバーグ Hambagu ——— 192
75 ナポリタン Naporitan ——— 194
76 コラム：喫茶店文化 ——— 196

6章 ご当地料理
Regional Cuisine

ご当地料理 Regional Cuisine ——— 198
77 ジンギスカン Jingisukan ——— 200
78 きりたんぽ Kiritanpo ——— 201
79 ちゃんこ鍋 Chanko Nabe ——— 202
80 サザエのつぼ焼き Grilled Turban Shell ——— 203
81 朴葉味噌 Hoba Miso ——— 204
82 治部煮 Jibuni ——— 205
83 ゆうべし Yubeshi ——— 206

84 京漬物 Kyoto-style pickles ——— 207
85 お好み焼き Okonomiyaki ——— 208
86 フグ Blowfish ——— 209
87 ちゃんぽん Chanpon ——— 210
88 ミミガー Mimiga ——— 211
89 コラム：精進料理 ——— 212
90 コラム：コンビニ ——— 213

本書の利用法

◆各テーマのイントロダクション

テーマにまつわる基本
データです。
数字やその他データか
ら日本の食文化を見て
みましょう。
※データの内容は日本
に関するものです。

無料ダウンロード音声
のファイル番号です。

外国人の気になるポイ
ントを3つのトピックで
紹介します。

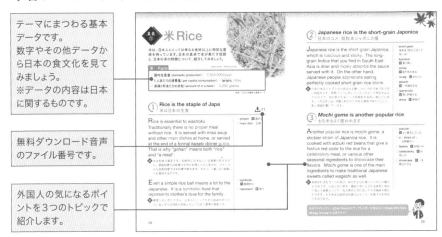

「カロリー（100ｇあたり）」と外食を想定した
おおよその「価格」情報です。

◆料理の紹介ページ

料理名です。
ローマ字読み／英語で
の説明の順に記載され
ています。

一目でどんな料理かイ
メージできる単語レベ
ルのキーワードです。
各料理を特徴づける食
材、調理法、調理器具・
器、味わいを紹介します。

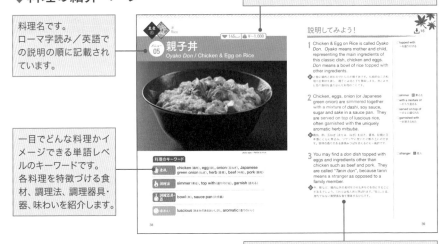

各料理の食材、レシピ、調理法などの基本情
報と豆知識を2〜3つのトピックで紹介します。

●本書特典「和食ガイドに使える！語彙・フレーズ集」を、Jリサーチ出版HP（https://www.jresearch.co.jp/book/b488034.html）よりご覧いただけます。

●音声ダウンロードの方法は、巻末ページをご覧ください。

和食の基本

The Basics of *Washoku*

和食とは？
What is *Washoku?*

和食とは？と聞かれたら、みなさんはどんなものを思い浮かべるでしょうか。ここでは、日本人の食文化の基本にある3つの特徴「シンプルさ」「熟練性」「適用力」について紹介していきます。

 Simplicity
シンプルさ

*S*ushi and *ramen* are the most well-known Japanese dishes outside Japan nowadays. These are very simple dishes made with only a few ingredients. Simplicity is the essence of Japanese cuisine.

☐ nowadays	副 今日
☐ ingredient	名 食材
☐ simplicity	名 シンプルさ
☐ cuisine	名 料理

訳 今日、海外で最も知られる日本料理は、鮨とラーメンです。これらの料理は数種の食材のみからつくられた、非常にシンプルな料理です。この簡素さは、和食の真髄なのです。

☐ addition	名 足し算
☐ subtraction	名 引き算
☐ layering	層
☐ showcase	動 際立たせる

*T*hey say French is the cuisine of addition, and Japanese is the cuisine of subtraction. Instead of layering flavors, Japanese cooks aim to minimize elements of the dish to showcase the flavors of seasonal ingredients.

訳 フランス料理は足し算、和食は引き算の料理であるといわれています。味を幾層にも重ねる代わりに、日本人の料理人は味の要素を最小限に抑え、旬の素材の風味を際立たせることを目指します。

② Craftsmanship
熟練性

Craftsmanship runs through Japanese cuisine. Many restaurants focus on one theme, such as *soba* and *yakitori*. As a result, cooks gain a deep understanding of the ingredients and techniques to make the dish perfectly. This is how the tradition is made.

□ **craftsmanship**
名 熟練性
□ **runs through**
〜を貫いている

 訳 熟練性は和食の根底に流れています。多くの飲食店が蕎麦や焼き鳥のように、食のテーマを一つに絞っています。その結果、料理人は食材や調理法への理解を深め、完成度の高い料理を生み出すことが可能になるのです。和食の伝統はこうして培われてきました。

③ Adaptability
適用力

On the other hand, Japanese people are surprisingly adaptable. For example, you can find French restaurants as classic as those in France all over the country. Regardless of the origin of the food, craftsmanship and tradition are highly respected in Japanese food culture.

□ **adaptable**
形 適用できる
□ **classic**
形 典型的な
□ **regardless of**
〜にかかわらず

 訳 その半面、日本人の適用性の高さにも驚かされます。例えばフランス本国に劣らぬような典型的なフランス料理店が、日本中に存在します。料理の起源にかかわらず、熟練性と伝統は、日本の食文化においてとても尊重されています。

自然の恵みと季節性
The Nature's Bounty and Seasonality

自然の豊かさから得られる多彩な食材は和食にとって欠かせないものです。旬の食材とともに四季を大事にする日本の食文化について紹介しましょう。

① The fertile land and the sea
肥沃な国土と海の恵み

The Japanese complex coastline is about 30,000km long. The cold nutrient-rich current *Oyashio* collides with the warm current *Kuroshio* off the eastern coast of Japan. These factors create an ideal fishing ground.

 日本の複雑な海岸線は３万キロメートルに及びます。冷たく栄養素の高い親潮が、日本の東側で暖かな黒潮とぶつかります。こうした要素が理想的な漁場を生み出します。

Japan is a small country, but the climate varies greatly from cool temperate in the north to subtropical in the south. Also, 70% of the land is covered by mountains and forests, which provide a diverse array of produce.

訳 日本は小さな国ですが、気候は冷涼な北から亜熱帯の南と多様です。また陸の70％は、多彩な食材を生む山岳と森林に覆われています。

□coastline
名 海岸線
□nutrient-rich
栄養豊富
□collide 動 ぶつかる
□fishing ground
漁場

□subtropical
形 亜熱帯の
□diverse array
多種多様な

② Distinct seasons
豊かな季節性

Seasonality is inherent in *washoku*, and the Japanese celebrate *shun*, the peak of flavor during the season, throughout the year.

訳 季節性は和食の重要な要素です。日本には季節の最高の風味「旬」をたたえる習慣があります。

□inherent 形 固有の
□celebrate 動 たたえる

For example, *kaiseki* is a multi-course dinner to feature *shun* along with seasonal tableware and décor.

訳 例えば会席は、器、しつらえと共に旬の素材を楽しむコース料理です。

□multi-course コース（料理の）
□tableware 名 器
□décor 名 しつらえ、装飾

Fatty flavorful pacific saury (*sanma*) comes to the market in early fall and many restaurants put up a sign "we are serving sanma", because its *shun* lasts only for a few weeks.

訳 脂ののった風味豊かな秋刀魚は初秋に出回り、その旬はほんの数週間だけなので、多くの飲食店が「秋刀魚あります」という看板を出します。

□fatty 形 脂ののった
□pacific saury サンマ
□put up a sign 看板を出す

In Japan there are 24 seasons that reflect *shun* in accordance with the ancient calendar.

訳 日本では古代の暦に基づき、旬を反映した24の季節が存在します。

□in accordance with ～と一致して

敬意と感謝
Respect and Gratitude

食材や料理に対して、敬意と感謝を示すことは和食の特徴です。「いただきます」「ごちそうさま」「もったいない」という日本ならではの表現について、紹介しましょう。

photo：Graphs / PIXTA（ピクスタ）

① *Itadakimasu* and *Gochisosama*
いただきます、ごちそうさま

3

If you pay attention to how the Japanese communicate, you will often notice respect and gratitude in their language and attitude. An example is the word *itadakimasu* (thank you for the precious food), which they always say before starting a meal.

☐ pay attention to
　～に注意を払う
☐ gratitude **名** 感謝

 訳 日本人のコミュニケーションの仕方を見てみると、敬意と感謝が言葉にも態度にも溢れていることがわかります。一例は、日本人が食べる前に必ず（貴重な食べ物への感謝を込めて）言う「いただきます」です。

It is expressed toward god or nature that provided the bounty, and also to whoever helped to make the meal such as family members, cooks, farmers and fishermen. *Gochisosama* is the word used after the meal to say "It was a wonderful feast."

☐ bounty **名** 恵み
☐ feast **名** ごちそう

 訳 神や自然が与えてくれた恵みに加え、その食事を作ってくれた家族や料理人、農民や漁師などすべてに対して向けられた言葉です。「ごちそうさま」は「素晴らしい食事をいただきました」と伝える言葉です。

② Mottainai
もったいない

*M*ottainai is another word that reflects the modest attitude of the Japanese. It means "we should not waste such a valuable thing, even when the 'thing' can be potentially thrown away".

訳 「もったいない」も日本人の謙虚な姿勢を象徴する言葉。「捨ててしまうこともありうるけれど、こんな貴重なものを無駄にしてはいけない」という意味です。

□ modest 形 謙虚な
□ potentially
　　副 もしかすると

*T*hat is why the whole fish and animal are widely eaten in *washoku*.

訳 そのため和食では素材を丸ごと食べることが一般的です。

*F*or example, *horumon-yaki* is grilled organ meats that could be discarded in other food cultures, but prized in Japan for its great taste and dense nutrients.

訳 例えばホルモン焼きは、他の食文化では捨てられてしまうような内臓を、その美味しさと栄養価の高さに着目し珍重する料理です。

□ discarded
　　動 捨てる
□ prize
　　動 珍重する
□ dense
　　形 密度の濃い
□ nutrient 名 栄養物

日本風のおもてなし
Omotenashi Japanese-style Hospitality

日本文化で重要視される「おもてなし」の考え方は、和食のいたるところにみられます。こうした価値観をよく反映している茶道についても紹介してみましょう。

① Genuine hospitality
純粋なホスピタリティ

 4

Respect and gratitude are the fundamental values in Japanese culture.

 敬意と感謝は日本文化の基盤にある価値です。

□ respect	名 敬意
□ gratitude	名 感謝

Omotenashi is the concept derived from them. It is a form of hospitality but is offered without expecting rewards.

訳 おもてなしはそれらに根ざした理念で、ホスピタリティの一つの形ではありますが、見返りを期待しないものです。

□ derived from	〜由来の
□ reward	名 見返り

For example, after dinner at a Japanese restaurant, the staff may come outside to see you off and keep bowing even after you disappear from their sight. It is a genuine gratitude for your visit.

訳 例えば和食店での食事の後、スタッフが店の外まで出て、お客の姿が見えなくなるまでお辞儀を続けることもあります。これはお客の訪問への純粋な感謝の表現です。

□ see off	見送る
□ bow	動 お辞儀する
□ genuine	形 純粋な

② Tea ceremony: The embodiment of *Omotenashi*
おもてなしを体現する茶道

You can find the essence of *Omotenashi* in Japanese tea ceremony (*Sado*). Each movement of the host is intended to make the guest comfortable and enjoy the moment.

□ be intended to
〜することを目的として

訳 茶道にはおもてなしの精神が凝縮されています。亭主の一つひとつの動きは客の居心地良さと楽しみを作り出すためのものです。

This idea is called *Ichigo Ichie*. The host views the gathering as an important event during one's lifetime that will never occur again, and serve the guests in the best way possible with omotenashi.

□ gathering
名 集まり
□ lifetime 名 生涯
□ possible with
〜が可能な

訳 この発想は「一期一会」と呼ばれます。亭主はその茶会を一生に一度しかない大切な出来事と考え、客に誠心誠意のおもてなしを尽くすという意味です。

The host's attention to details, such as perfect temperature of the tea, carefully selected teacups and seasonal flowers in the room, is his/her expression of *omotenashi*.

□ detail 名 細部
□ temperature
名 温度

訳 完璧なお茶の温度、丁寧に選んだ茶器、部屋に飾る旬の花など亭主の細微にいたる心配りは、亭主のおもてなしの表現です。

一汁三菜
Ichiju Sansai

和食の基本コンセプト「一汁三菜」に馴染みのない外国人も多いでしょう。一汁三菜の原則や、メリットについて紹介してみましょう。

photo：tojiko ／ PIXTA (ピクスタ)

 One soup, three dishes
一汁三菜

5

The classic Japanese meal consists of one soup, one main dish and two side dishes that are always served with a bowl of rice and pickles. This format is called *ichiju sansai*. Since rice and pickles are essential items in *washoku*, they are not even included in the term.

訳 伝統的な日本の食事は汁物一品、主菜一品、副菜２二品にいつもご飯一杯と漬物が添えられています。この形は一汁三菜と呼ばれます。米と漬物は和食において不可欠な料理なのでその名前に含まれていません。

You can find the format of *ichiju sansai* on breakfast, lunch and dinner menus. Made with seasonal vegetables and nutritious protein, *ichiju sansai* offers a healthy meal throughout the day.

訳 一汁三菜は朝食、昼食、夕食の各メニューに見られます。旬の野菜と栄養価の高いたんぱく質で作られた一汁三菜は、１日を通して健康的な食事を提供してくれます。

□consist of
　〜で構成される
□main dish　主菜
□side dish　副菜
□pickle　名 漬物

□format　名 形式
□protein
　名 たんぱく質

② Delicious and Satisfying
美味しく満足

At the table, soup is always placed on your right, rice on the left, pickles in the middle, the main dish on the far right, and the side dishes on the far left next to each other.

訳 食卓では、いつも汁物は右手、米は左、漬物はその間、主菜は奥右手、副菜は奥左手に並べて置かれます。

The proper way to eat *ichiju sansai* is to rotate the dishes. Start with the soup, have a bite of rice, have a bite of the main dish and so on.

訳 正しく食べる順序は、まず汁を飲み、ご飯、主菜、といったように、各品を交互に食べること。

□rotate **動** 循環する

In this way, you can enjoy the taste of each dish, maximize satisfaction and avoid overeating.

訳 そうすることで、それぞれの料理を楽しんで満喫しながら過食を防ぐことができます。

□overeat **動** 食べすぎる

15

五味五色五法
Gomi Goshoku Goho

「五味五色五法」は、五つの味、五つの色、五つの調理法のことです。一見難しそうな言葉ですが、和食の魅力の根底にある大原則なので、紹介してみましょう。

photo：グレーチャート / PIXTA (ピクスタ)

① Five tastes, five colors, five methods
五味五色五法

6

□principle　名 原則

There is an important principle in cooking *washoku* called *gomi goshoku goho*(five tastes, five colors, five cooking methods). It means five tastes, five colors, five cooking methods.

 訳 和食の調理には五味五色五法という大事な原則があります。これは五つの味、五つの色、五つの調理法という意味です。

The five tastes are sweet, spicy, salty, bitter and sour.

訳 五味は甘味、辛味、塩気、苦味、酸味。

The five colors are red, green, yellow, white and black.

訳 五色は、赤、緑、黄、白、黒。

The five methods are *yaku* (roast/bake), *niru* (boil/simmer), *musu* (steam), *ageru* (deep-fry) and *nama* (raw).

訳 五法は焼く、煮る、蒸す、揚げる、生です。

② Beautiful and balanced meal
美しくバランスの良い食事

The five tastes offer an enjoyable and satisfying meal. With the five colors you can make aesthetic dishes that increase appetite. Also, since each color represents different types of nutrition, colorful dishes are highly nourishing as well. With the five cooking methods you can maximize nutrition and flavors of various ingredients.

□ aesthetic
形 美しい

□ appetite 名 食欲

□ nourishing
形 滋養になる

訳 五味は味わい深く満足度の高い食事を生み出します。五色を使えば食欲を湧かせる美しい料理を作ることができます。またそれぞれの色が異なる栄養素を示すため、彩り豊かな料理は滋養が豊かでもあるのです。五法を使えば様々な素材の栄養素の価値と風味を最大に引き出すことができます。

③ The "five" principles and *omotenashi*
「五」の原則とおもてなし

There are two other sets of fives in *washoku*: *gokan*, five-sensitivity (sight, hearing, smell, feel, and taste) and *goteki*, five-adequacy, (right temperature, ingredient, volume, technique and attitude).

□ sensitivity
名 感受性

□ adequacy
名 適切さ

□ volume 名 量

訳 さらに二つの「五」の原則があります。五感 (見る、聞く、嗅ぐ、触れる、味わう) と五適 (最適な温度、食材、量、調理法、気遣い) です。

Cooks keep these elements in mind to make the guests' experience a great one. The "five" principles are closely connected to the *omotenashi* spirit.

□ in mind 念頭に

訳 客の体験を最高のものにする為料理人はこれらの要素を念頭に置きます。これらの「五」の原則はおもてなし精神と直結しています。

栄養豊富な和食
Washoku is nutritious

和食は健康的だと言われる理由には、発酵食品や旨味をふんだんに使う料理や、食べ物をまるごと食べて栄養を無駄にしない「一物全体」の考えが根付いているからともいえます。

photo：I / PIXTA (ピクスタ)

The rich culture of fermented foods
豊かな発酵食品文化

*W*ashoku is highly nutritious thanks to the principles of *ichiju sansai* and *gomi goshoku goho*. There are other reasons why *washoku* is so healthy.

□ thanks to
〜のおかげで

> **訳** 和食は一汁三菜や五味五色五法の原則のおかげでとても栄養豊かです。その他にも和食が健康的な理由があります。

T he Japanese eat many fermented foods such as *miso*, soy sauce and *natto*. Fermented foods contain beneficial bacteria that can improve digestion and boost immunity.

□ contain
動 〜を含む
□ bacteria 名 菌
□ digestion 名 消化
□ boost 動 高める
□ immunity
名 免疫性

> **訳** 日本人は味噌、醤油、納豆ほか様々な発酵食品を食します。発酵食品には多くの有益な菌が含まれており、消化や免疫性を高めます。

② The power of *umami*
旨味の力

I n addition to the basic five tastes, the 6th taste called *umami* is important in *washoku*. *Dashi* and fermented foods are very rich in *umami*. Because it provides a delicious savory taste, you can reduce an excessive use of salt and other seasonings to satisfy your palate.

□ fermented
形 発酵した
□ savory
形 風味豊かな
□ excessive
形 過度の
□ seasoning
名 調味料
□ palate　名 味覚

 訳 和食には基本的な五味に加え、旨味という6つ目の味が重要な役割を果たします。旨味は出汁や発酵食品に豊富に含まれています。美味しく風味豊かな旨味には、塩など他の調味料の過度な使用を防ぐ効果もあります。

③ Eat the whole
一物全体

I n Japan, *Ichibutsu Zentai*, or eating the whole food, is believed to be a wonderful way to absorb nutrition. For example, the Japanese eat vitamin-rich skin and leaves of root vegetables, and fry calcium-rich fish bones to make a tasty garnish or a snack.

□ absorb
動 吸収する
□ root vegetable
根菜
□ garnish　名 薬味

 訳 日本では食べ物を丸ごと食べる「一物全体」が優れた栄養摂取の方法とされています。例えば日本人は、ビタミンが豊富な根菜の皮や葉を食べ、カルシウムをたっぷり含んだ魚の骨を揚げて薬味やおやつにします。

M ottainai is related to the idea of *Ichibutsu Zentai*.

訳 「もったいない」の理念はこの一物全体の発想にもつながっています。

出汁
Dashi / Japanese Stock

旨味のカギを握る出汁は和食の要です。材料のブレンドで
旨味がパワーアップする料理の科学まで紹介できたら、中々
のものです。

photo：jazzman / PIXTA（ピクスタ）

① *Dashi* is the foundation of *washoku*
出汁は和食の基本　　　　　　　　8

Dashi, (Japanese stock) is the foundation
of *washoku*. The main ingredients are
kombu (kelp), *katsuobushi* (cured bonito),
niboshi (small dried fish) and dried
shiitake mushroom.

☐ foundation
　名 基本
☐ cured　形 燻製の
☐ dried　形 乾燥の

訳 和食の（スープ）ストックは出汁と呼ばれ、和食の基本です。
昆布、鰹節、煮干し、乾燥椎茸などが主な材料です。

② *Kombu / Katsuobushi / Niboshi* / Dried *Shiitake*
昆布・鰹節・煮干し・乾燥椎茸

After being soaked in water and heated
up to just before boiling point, *kombu*
imparts the clean, deep flavors to the
liquid. To make katsuobushi, the fish is
simmered, deboned, smoke-dried and
cured with beneficial mold that increases
umami. Shaved katsuobushi looks like
beautiful flavorful ribbons.

☐ soak in　～に浸す
☐ heat up　加熱する
☐ boiling point　沸点
☐ impart　動 与える
☐ simmered　形 煮た
☐ deboned
　形 骨を抜いた
☐ smoke-dried
　形 燻製にした
☐ shaved　形 削った

訳 水にしばらく浸け沸騰寸前まで煮ると、昆布はすっきりとした
奥深い香りを生み出します。鰹節を作るには、鰹を茹でて骨抜
きし、燻して乾燥させ、旨味を増す有益なカビをつけ、加工し
ます。削ると美しく香り高いリボン状になります。

Niboshi is made of small fish such as anchovies, round herring and flying fish. It adds an deep oceanic flavor to dashi.

 煮干しはカタクチイワシ、ウルメイワシ、アゴなどの小魚で作られます。海を思わせる風味を醸します。

□ **anchovy**
　名 カタクチイワシ
□ **round herring**
　名 ウルメイワシ
□ **flying fish**　名 アゴ

*Dried *shiitake* gives an earthy aroma, reminiscent of the forest floor, to dashi. It is particularly useful in vegetarian *Shojin ryori* (p.212).

 乾燥椎茸は森の土の香りを伝えるような独特の風味を生み出します。ことに野菜のみを使う精進料理によく使われます。

□ **earthy**　形 土の
□ **reminiscent**
　形 〜を思い出させるような

③ Multiplying *umami*
旨味の相乗効果

*Most *dashi* is made with a few ingredients, because the level of *umami* multiplies by combining different amino acids in them.

 各素材に含まれる異なるアミノ酸の組み合せが旨味の相乗効果を生み出すため、大半の出汁は複数の素材で作られています。例えば出汁を昆布（グルタミン酸が豊富）と鰹節（イノシン酸が豊富）で作ると、旨味は単独で作る7−8倍になります。

□ **multiply**
　動 相乗させる
□ **amino acids**
　アミノ酸

*For example, dashi made with *kombu* (glutamic acid), and *katsuobushi* (inosinic acid) has 7-8 times more *umami* than *dashi* made with a single ingredient.

 例えば出汁を昆布（グルタミン酸が豊富）と鰹節（イノシン酸が豊富）で作ると、旨味は単独で作る7−8倍になります。

□ **glutamic acid**
　グルタミン酸
□ **inosinic acid**
　イノシン酸

調味料 Seasonings

和食の調味料の中には醤油や味噌など海外で知られ
ているものも多い反面、作り方や効能など、実は日本人
でもよく知らなかったりしますね。

① 醤油 *Shoyu* / Soy sauce

9

How to make *shoyu* 醤油のつくりかた

Soy sauce is a primary seasoning of *washoku*. Traditionally steamed soybeans and roasted wheat are mixed with *koji* mold and salt, and fermented for several months or longer.

□mold 名菌
□seasoning 名調味料
□steam 動蒸す
□roast 動炒る
□ferment 動発酵させる

 訳 醤油は和食の基本の調味料の１つです。伝統的には蒸した大豆と炒った小麦を、麹菌と塩とともに最低数ヶ月発酵させて作ります。

Three types of *shoyu* 3種類の醤油

The most popular type is *koikuchi*. *Usukuchi* is saltier than *koikuchi* but has a lighter color, which is convenient to highlight the color of food. It is popular in the Kansai area. *Tamari* is made with a little or no wheat. The taste is more intense and rich in *umami* with a thicker mouth feel.

□highlight 動強調する
□intense 形強烈な
□thick 形とろみがある
□mouth feel 名口当たり

 訳 もっとも一般的な種類は濃口です。薄口は濃口より塩辛く色が薄いため、食材の色を生かしたい料理に便利。関西地方でよく見られます。溜は少量の小麦もしくは無使用で作られ、他の種類より濃厚で旨味が強く、とろみのある口当たりです。

② 味噌 *Miso* /Fermented Soybean Paste

Types of *miso*　味噌の種類

*M*iso is an important seasoning in
washoku. All *miso* is made with soybeans
and *koji*.

> **訳** 味噌は和食における重要な調味料の一つです。全ての味噌は大
> 豆と麹で作られています。

□barley　名 大麦

*M*ame miso is made with soybeans(*mame*)
only (popular in Nagoya). If rice (*kome*) is
added, it is called *kome miso*, the most
common type. With barley (*mugi*), it is
called *mugi miso* (popular in Kyushu).

> **訳** 豆だけで作られたものは豆味噌（名古屋に多い）、米を加えたも
> のを米味噌（最も一般的）、麦を加えたものが麦味噌（九州に多
> い）です。

Factors of color and sweetness　色と甘さの決め手

*M*iso has a wide range of colors and
level of sweetness depending on how
long it was fermented (the longer, the
darker) and how much *koji* mold was
used (the more *koji* mold, the sweeter).

> **訳** 味噌の色と甘さは発酵期間（長いほど濃い色）と麹の使用量（多
> いほど甘い）により幅があります。

□range　名 範囲
□depending on
　~による

photo：kai / PIXTA (ピクスタ)

23

③ 酢 Vinegar

Rice vinegar (*komezu*) is the preferred vinegar in Japan. It is milder and sweeter than other types of vinegar. Rice vinegar is used in many dishes, such as *sushi* rice and Japanese-style quick pickles, and meat dishes to reduce fattiness.

□ preferred
形 望ましい
□ fattiness 名 脂肪質

訳 日本で多用される酢は米酢です。他の種類の酢に比べまろやかで甘みがあります。米酢は鮨米や酢の物、さっぱり感を与える肉料理ほか多彩な料理に使われています。

photo：freeangle / PIXTA (ピクスタ)

④ 日本酒 Japanese *Sake*

Sake is the national alcohol beverage of Japan. It is delicious and flavorful as a beverage, and also very handy in cooking.

□ handy 形 重宝な
□ unwanted
形 不快な
□ odor 名 匂い
□ texture 名 食感

訳 酒は日本の国酒 です。味わい豊かな美味しい飲み物であるばかりか、料理においてもとても重宝します。

For instance, *sake* can remove unwanted odor like fishiness, soften texture of food and increase *umami*.

訳 例えば、酒は魚臭さなどの匂いを除いたり、食材を柔らかくしたり、旨味を高めてくれます。

photo：motoko / PIXTA (ピクスタ)

⑤ みりん *Mirin*

*M*irin is a sweet cooking liquid with around 14% alcohol. It is made with sticky rice, *koji* and added distilled alcohol such as *shochu*.

訳 みりんは米、麹に焼酎などの蒸留酒を加えた、アルコール度数14%前後の料理酒です。

☐ distilled alcohol
蒸留酒

*M*irin helps to create a dish with deep and complex taste, because the alcohol has an ability to penetrate into food together with other flavor elements.

訳 アルコールが風味を食材に深く浸透させる効果を持つため、砂糖に比べより深く複雑な味に仕上げてくれる特性があります。

☐ penetrate into
〜に浸透させる
☐ together with
〜とともに

*M*irin is also used to glaze food to give a beautiful shine.

訳 みりんは料理に美しい照りをつけることにも使われます。

☐ glaze 動 つやをだす
☐ shine 名 照り

*M*irin is an ingredient of *Toso*, spiced medicinal *sake* that is drunk during the New Year celebration to ward off illness.

訳 みりんは新年の祝いで飲まれる、病を避けるための薬用酒「屠蘇」の食材の一つでもあります。

☐ medicinal 形 薬用
☐ ward off
〜を避ける

photo：kai / PIXTA (ピクスタ)

⑥ 薬味 *Yakumi*; Japanese Herbs & Spices

Utility of *yakumi* 薬味の効用

Herbs and spices called *yakumi* can play a major role in elevating delicious flavor of *washoku*, which tend to consist of only a few ingredients. *Yakumi* also offers health benefits such as boosting appetite and helping digestion.

□ play role in
　～で役割を果たす
□ boost 動 高める
□ appetite 名 食欲
□ digestion 名 消化

訳 和食は各食材の風味を生かすため、限られた数の食材から作られています。そのため香草や香辛料などの薬味は料理全体の味わいをぐんと引き立てます。薬味は食欲を高めたり消化を助けるなどの健康効果も持っています。

Types of *yakumi* 薬味の種類

Vegetable *yakumi* includes *shiso*, *wasabi*, *sansho* and *togarashi*. There are fruit *yakumi*, such as *umeboshi* (pickled plum), *yuzu* and *sudachi* citrus. Fish can be *yakumi*, e.g. bonito flakes and *sakura* shrimp. A classic dish that features *yakumi* is chilled *tofu* topped with ginger and bonito flakes. Another is grilled *unagi* (eel) sprinkled with *sansho* pepper.

□ citrus 名 かんきつ
　類
□ e.g. 略 例えば
□ bonito flakes 鰹節
□ shrimp 名 えび
□ chilled
　形 冷やされた
□ sprinkle with
　～をふりかける

訳 野菜系の薬味は紫蘇、ミョウガ、わさび、山椒、唐辛子。梅干し、ゆず、すだちは果実系。鰹節と桜えびは魚介類です。薬味を使った代表的な料理の一つは豆腐の生姜を添えた冷奴や、山椒をふりかけた鰻です。

photo：my room / PIXTA (ピクスタ)

2章

定番の和食

Popular Dishes of *Washoku*

米 Rice

米は、日本人にとっては単なる食材以上に特別な意味を持っています。日本の食卓で米が果たす役割と、日本の米の特徴について、紹介してみましょう。

photo：ぱりろく / PIXTA（ピクスタ）

米—Facts

- 国内生産量（domestic production）—7,924,000t/year
- 1人あたりの消費量（per capita consumption）— 🍚🍚🍚 /day
- 茶碗1杯あたりの米粒（amount of in a bowl）—3,250 grains

参照：2018 年農林水産省データ

① Rice is the staple of Japan
米は日本の主食

11

Rice is essential to *washoku*.
Traditionally there is no proper meal
without rice. It is served with *miso* soup
and other main dishes at home, or served
at the end of a formal *kaiseki* dinner (p.101).
That is why "*gohan*" means both "rice"
and "a meal".

□ proper 形 適切な
□ main dish 主食

 米は和食の基本です。伝統的には米なしには食事と呼びません。家庭料理では味噌汁や他の料理とともに供され、フォーマルな会席料理では米料理で締めます。だから「ご飯」は「食事」とも意味するのです。

Even a simple rice ball means a lot to the
Japanese. It is a symbolic food that
represents mother's love for the family.

□ symbolic
　形 象徴的な
□ represent 動 表す

 簡素なおにぎりですら、日本人にとって大きな価値を持つもの。おにぎりは母親が家族に対して込めた愛情の象徴です。

② Japanese rice is the short-grain Japonica
日本のコメ、短粒米ジャポニカ種

Japanese rice is the short-grain *Japonica*, which is luscious and sticky. The long-grain *Indica* that you find in South East Asia is drier and nicely absorbs the sauce served with it. On the other hand, Japanese people appreciate eating perfectly cooked short grain rice alone.

 日本の米はジャポニカと呼ばれる艶（つや）のある粘り気の高い短粒米です。南西アジアに多いインディカという長粒米はよりドライで、共に供されるソースを吸収するのに適しています。一方日本人は、完璧に炊かれた白米を単独で味わうことに、高い価値を置いています。

- □ short-grain
  単粒米（粒が小さくて短い米）
- □ luscious
  形 香り高い
- □ sticky
  形 粘り気がある
- □ nicely 副 きちんと
- □ absorb
  動 〜を吸収する
- □ appreciate
  動 高く評価する
- □ alone 副 単独で

③ *Mochi gome* is another popular rice
もち米もよく使われます

Another popular rice is *mochi gome*, a stickier strain of *Japonica* rice. It is cooked with *adzuki* red beans that give a festive red color to the rice for a celebratory meal, or various other seasonal ingredients to showcase their flavors. *Mochi gome* is one of the main ingredients to make traditional Japanese sweets called *wagashi* as well.

 多用されるもう一つの米は、粘りがさらに強いジャポニカ種のもち米です。小豆と共に炊き、縁起が良いとされる赤色に染めて祝いの食事としたり、旬の素材と共に炊いてその風味を際立たせます。もち米は伝統的な和食のスイーツ、和菓子の主原料でもあります。

- □ popular
  形 よく普及している
- □ a… strain of ~
  …な特徴の〜
- □ festive 形 お祝いの
- □ celebratory 形 お祝いの
- □ showcase 動 〜を際立たせる

米はグルテンフリー (glten free) なので、アレルギーを抱える人 (those who have allergy issues) にも使えます！

29

 米
Rice

165kcal

 メニュー 01

ご飯の炊き方
How to Cook Rice

photo：kai / PIXTA（ピクスタ）

料理のキーワード

 食材　short grain rice（単粒米）

 調理法　rinse（研ぐ）, soak（浸す）, boil（ゆでる）/ cook（炊く）steam（蒸す）, fluff（空気を入れる）

 調理器具・器　pot（鍋）, lid（蓋）, bowl（茶碗）

 味わい　fluffy（ふんわり）, shiny（つやつや）

1 Making fluffy, shiny, perfectly cooked rice is something the Japanese take pride in. It is not easy to master, but the process of cooking rice is simple. You can use a rice cooker, but manually cooked rice tastes much better!

□ fluffy 形 ふわふわの
□ take pride in 〜を誇る
□ rice cooker 炊飯器
□ manually 形 手作業で

訳 ふわふわとした輝きのある、完璧に炊かれたご飯は日本人が誇るもの。熟練の域に達するのは容易ではありませんが、調理法はとてもシンプルです。炊飯器を使うこともできますが、自分の手で炊いたご飯はずっと美味しくなります！

2 Measure the rice. Rinse it a few times until the water becomes almost clear. Add fresh water and soak it for 30 minutes and drain. Put the rice in a pot with a heavy lid and add water (1.3 cup of water for 1 cup of rice).

□ rinse 動 米を研ぐ
□ soak 動 浸す
□ drain 動 水を切る
□ lid 名 ふた

訳 短粒米をボウルに入れて水が濁らなくなるまで数回研ぎます。きれいな水を加えて30分ほど浸し、水を切ります。米を重めのふたのついた鍋に入れ、水を加えます（1カップの米に1/3カップの水）。

3 Cover the pot with the lid and boil it for 15 minutes. Let the rice cool off for 10 minutes. Fluff the rice with a rice paddle or a fork to improve texture.

□ cool off 火からおろす
□ fluff 動 空気をいれる
□ rice paddle しゃもじ

訳 鍋に蓋をし15分強、茹でます。火から下ろして10分ほど蒸し、食感を高めるためにしゃもじやフォークなどでふんわり空気を入れます。

 140kcal

ご飯もの（炊き込みご飯）
Gohan Mono (Takikomi Gohan) / Rice Dishese

photo：ささざわ / PIXTA（ピクスタ）

料理のキーワード

 食材
rice（米）, bamboo shoot（竹の子）, chestnut（栗）,
mushroom（きのこ）, sea bream（鯛）

 調理法
cook（炊く）

説明してみよう！

↓13

1 *Gohan mono* means rice dishes that are cooked with other ingredients. There are mainly three types: *takikomi gohan*, *maze gohan* and *okowa*.

訳 ご飯ものとはご飯を他の素材と一緒に炊いた料理のことです。炊き込みご飯、混ぜご飯、おこわが主な種類です。

□mainly 副 主に

2 *Takikomi gohan* is rice cooked with other ingredients along with *dashi* and seasoning. In some regions, it is called *gomoku gohan* or *kayaku gohan*.

訳 炊き込みご飯は出汁とその他の素材とともに炊いたもの。地方により五目ご飯、かやく御飯とも呼ばれます。

□along with
　〜と一緒に

3 *Takikomi gohan* often showcases the seasonal ingredients. For example, in spring takikomi *gohan* made with *takenoko* (bamboo shoots) is something Japanese people look forward to every year. In fall, chestnut and *matsutake* mushroom are the classic ingredients.

訳 炊き込みご飯は旬の素材をテーマにしたものがよく見られます。例えば春の筍ご飯は日本人が毎年待ちわびるもの。秋には栗や松茸などが代表的な素材です。

□look forward to
　〜を待ちわびる
□chestnut 名 栗

混ぜご飯 **200**kcal / おこわ **190**kcal

ご飯もの（混ぜご飯 & おこわ）
Gohan Mono (Maze Gohan & Okowa) / Rice Dishese

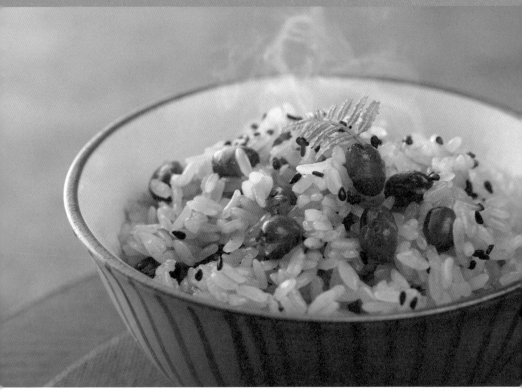

photo：jazzman / PIXTA（ピクスタ）

料理のキーワード

 食材　sticky short grain rice（もち米）**,** *shiso* leaf（紫蘇）**,**
scallop（ホタテ）**,** *adzuki* bean（小豆）

 調理法　boil 茹でる **/** cook（炊く）**,** steam（蒸す）**,**
mix into already cooked rice（炊いたご飯に混ぜる）

説明してみよう！

 14

1 *Maze gohan* is similar to *takikomi gohan*. Iingredients are mixed into already cooked rice to make *maze gohan*, whereas rice and other ingredients are cooked together to make *takikomi gohan*. *Maze gohan* is suitable for ingredients that could lose flavor or texture if they were cooked with rice, such as fresh *shiso* leaves and delicate scallops.

□is similar to
　〜に似ている
□mix into
　〜に混ぜ合わせる
□whereas
　接 である一方で
□is suitable for
　〜に向いている
□delicate 形 繊細な
□scallop 名 ホタテ貝

訳 混ぜご飯は炊き込みご飯と似ています。米と他の素材が一緒に炊かれるのが炊き込みご飯。一方すでに炊かれたご飯に他の食材を混ぜて作るのが混ぜご飯です。混ぜご飯は、たとえばフレッシュな紫蘇の葉や繊細なホタテなどといった、米と一緒に炊くと風味や食感を損なう食材を使う際に適しています。

2 *Okowa* is different from *takikomi gohan* or *maze gohan*. *Okowa* is made with *mochi gome*, sticky short grain rice. Also, *okowa* is steamed instead of boiled.

□instead of　代わりに

訳 おこわは炊き込みご飯とも混ぜご飯とも異なります。まずおこわはもち米を使用します。そして米は茹でる代わりに蒸します。

3 *Okowa* can mean *sekihan* (red rice), which is a type of *okowa* cooked with red *adzuki* beans. Since red represents divinity and festivity, it is often served at weddings, birthdays and other celebratory occasions.

□divinity 名 神聖
□festivity 名 お祝い
□celebratory
　occasions
　祝いの席

訳 おこわは赤飯（赤いご飯）を意味することもあります。赤は神聖でおめでたい色とされるため、赤飯は結婚式や誕生日などの祝いの席によく楽しまれる料理です。

35

主食
①

米
Rice

お茶漬け 75kcal / 雑炊 140kcal

メニュー
04

お茶漬け、雑炊
Ochazuke & Zosui / Rice-base Soup

photo：ささざわ / PIXTA（ピクスタ）

料理のキーワード

 食材   rice（米）, tea（茶）, topping（具材）, pickled vegetable（漬物）, seaweed（海苔）, fish（魚）/ soups（汁）

 調理法   submerge（浸す）/ cook（煮込む）

 調理器具・器   bowl（茶碗）/ hot pot（鍋）

1 *Ochazuke* is a bowl of rice submerged in tea. The history goes back to the *Edo* period (17th -19th centuries) when tea became a part of the public's diet.

訳 お茶漬けはお茶にご飯を浸したものです。その歴史は、お茶が庶民の日常食の一部となった江戸時代 (17-19世紀) に遡ります。

□ submerge in	～に浸す
□ go back to	～にさかのぼる
□ diet 名 日常食	

2 Over time, various toppings were added such as pickled vegetables, seaweed and fish. As a result, *ochazuke* became a quick, easy and economical dish to be enjoyed as a meal or a snack.

訳 時代を経て、野菜の漬物、海藻、魚など多彩な具を盛り込むようになりました。その結果、お茶漬けは素早く簡単で手頃な料理となり、食事や間食として楽しまれるようになりました。

□ over time	時代を経て
□ seaweed 名 海藻	
□ snack 名 間食	

3 *Zosui* is made with rice, *dashi*, seasonings and various ingredients. It is common to make *zosui* by adding cooked rice to the leftover soup in a hot pot. Since the rice absorbs all the *umami* in the pot, you don't waste anything. This is an example of the "*mottainai*" spirit.

訳 雑炊は米、出汁、調味料と様々な素材で作られています。鍋料理の残りの汁に炊いた米を加えて作るのも一般的です。米が鍋のすべてのうま味を吸収するので無駄を一切避けることができます。これは「もったいない」の精神の一例です。

□ leftover 形 残りの	
□ absorb 動 ～を吸収する	
□ waste 動 無駄にする	
□ spirit 名 精神	

主食① 米 Rice

🍚 145kcal　👛 ¥〜1,000

メニュー 05

親子丼
Oyako Don / Chicken & Egg on Rice

photo：aijiro / PIXTA（ピクスタ）

料理のキーワード

 食材
chicken（鶏肉）, egg（卵）, onion（玉ねぎ）, Japanese green onion（ねぎ）, herb（香草）, beef（牛肉）, pork（豚肉）

 調理法
simmer（煮る）, top with（盛り付ける）, garnish（添える）

 調理器具・器
bowl（丼）, sauce pan（片手鍋）

 味わい
luscious（あまみのあるおいしさ）, aromatic（香りのいい）

38

1 Chicken & Egg on Rice is called *Oyako Don*. *Oyako* means mother and child, representing the main ingredients of this classic dish, chicken and eggs. *Don* means a bowl of rice topped with other ingredients.

訳 ご飯に鶏肉と卵をのせたものが親子丼です。伝統的なこの料理の主素材を表し、親子とは母と子を意味します。丼とは米に他の食材を盛り込んだ料理のことです。

□ topped with
　〜を盛り付ける

2 Chicken, eggs, onion (or Japanese green onion) are simmered together with a mixture of *dashi*, soy sauce, sugar and *sake* in a sauce pan. They are served on top of luscious rice, often garnished with the uniquely aromatic herb *mitsuba*.

訳 鶏肉、卵、玉ねぎ（または、ねぎ）を出汁、醤油、砂糖と日本酒とともに煮込み、ツヤツヤに炊いたご飯の上にのせます。独特の香りのある香草みつばを添えるのも一般的です。

□ simmer　動 煮込む
□ with a mixture of
　〜が入り混ざる
□ served on top of
　〜の上に盛られた
□ garnished with
　〜が添えられた

3 You may find a *don* dish topped with eggs and ingredients other than chicken such as beef and pork. They are called "*Tanin don*", because tanin means a stranger as opposed to a family member.

訳 牛、豚など、鶏肉以外の具材をのせた丼ものを目にすることがあるでしょう。これらは他人丼と呼ばれます。「他人」とは、身内ではない無関係な者を意味するからです。

□ stranger　名 他人

 170kcal ¥〜2,000

メニュー 06

天丼
Tendon / Tempura on Rice

photo：ささざわ / PIXTA（ピクスタ）

料理のキーワード

 食材　rice（米）, batter（衣）, fritter（衣をつけた揚げ物）, dipping sauce（たれ）

 調理法　top with（盛り付ける）, pour over（かける）, dip in（つける）

 味わい　juicy（汁気のある）

説明してみよう！

1 *Tendon* (*tempura* on rice) is an abbreviation of *tempura don* (rice topped with other ingredients). Hot *tempura* is put on top of hot rice, and is typically served with a sauce made with *dashi*, soy sauce, *mirin* and sugar.

訳 天丼（米の上に盛った天ぷら）とは天ぷら丼（丼とは他の食材を米に盛った料理）の略語です。熱いご飯の上に熱い天ぷらをのせ、出汁、醤油、みりん、砂糖をあわせたたれと一緒に出されます。

Commonly the sauce is poured over *tempura*, but in the traditional Edo-style, tempura is quickly dipped in the hot sauce to make it juicier.

訳 たれは通常天ぷらの上にかけられますが、伝統的な江戸流では、熱いつけ汁に天ぷらをさっと入れ、汁気の多さを楽しみます。

2 *Tempura* is a classic dish of *washoku*, but it was originally brought to Japan by the Portuguese in 16th century. The Japanese modified the original fritter and made it into a unique dish by using a thin batter and adding a dipping sauce.

訳 天ぷらは和食を代表する料理ですが、もともと16世紀にポルトガル人が日本にもたらしたものです。日本人が原型のフリッターに手を加え、薄い衣に変えつけ汁を加えて独自の料理に仕立てました。

□ abbreviation
　名 略語
□ pour over
　〜に注ぐ
□ juicy　形 汁気がある

□ Portuguese
　名 ポルトガル人
□ modifiy
　動 手を加える
□ fritter　動 フリッター
　（衣をつけて揚げた料理）
□ make 〜 into…
　〜を…にする
□ thin　形 薄い
□ dipping sauce
　付け汁

米
Rice

🍚 150kcal 👛 ¥100〜/巻、時価 market price

メニュー
07

鮨
Sushi / Sushi

photo：HN Photography / PIXTA（ピクスタ）

料理のキーワード

 食材
rice（米）, rice vinegar（米酢）, seafood（魚介類）, *nori* seaweed（海苔）, egg（卵）, vegetable（野菜）/ deep-fried *tofu* skin（油揚げ）

 調理法
roll（巻く）/ wrap（包む）/ hand-shape（手で形作る）/ scatter（散らす）/ press（押す）/ stuff（詰める）

 調理器具・器
bamboo mat（巻きす）

42

1 There are different types of *sushi*. *Nigiri* is a slice of raw seafood over *sushi* rice. It is typically prepared by skilled chefs at *sushi* restaurants. *Makimono* means rolled *sushi* wrapped in *nori* seaweed using a bamboo mat. Hand-shaped rolls are called *temaki*.

□ wrapped in
　〜に包まれた
□ bamboo mat
　巻きす
□ hand-shaped
　手で形を作られた

訳 鮨には色々な種類があります。握りは鮨飯に薄く切った生の魚介をのせたもので、通常、鮨の専門店で熟練した料理人が作ります。巻物とは海苔にのせ巻きすで巻いた鮨のことです。手で巻いたものは手巻きと呼びます。

2 *Chirashi* is a big bowl of *sushi* rice "scatterd"(= *chirashi*) with a variety of seafood, eggs and vegetables. *Hakozushi* (or *oshizushi*) is made by pressing rice and seafood in a box. It is popular in Osaka. *Inari zushi* is *sushi* rice stuffed inside a pouch of deep-fried sweet *tofu* skin.

□ scatterd
　散らばった
□ pouch　**名** 袋

訳 ちらしとは大きな器に多彩な魚介類、卵、野菜を「散らばった」ものです。箱鮨 (または押し鮨) は箱にご飯と魚介類を詰めて圧力をかけたもの。大阪で人気の種類です。稲荷鮨は甘い油揚げに鮨米を詰めたものです。

3 *Sushi* rice is as important as fish for *sushi* chefs, but it is made with just a few ingredients: short grain rice, rice vinegar, sugar and salt.

訳 鮨飯は鮨職人にとって魚と同等に重要なものですが、短粒米、米酢、砂糖と塩の、たった数種の素材から作られます。

 主食 ① 米
Rice

 235kcal /個

メニュー
08

餅
Mochi / Rice Cake

photo：june. / PIXTA（ピクスタ）

料理のキーワード

 食材
rice cake（餅）/ sticky short grain rice（もち米）, *nori* seaweed（海苔）, soy bean flour（きなこ）, *adzuki* bean paste（あんこ）, ice cream（アイス）

 調理法
pound（つく）, toast（こんがり焼く）, dip in（つける）, wrap in（包む）, dust with（まぶす）, coat with（覆う）

 味わい
crispy（パリッとした）

44

説明してみよう！

19

1 *Mochi* is a rice cake made by pounding sticky short grain rice, *mochi gome*. *Mochi* ice cream has become very popular worldwide, but it is a very recent product. Traditionally *mochi* is hand-pounded at a festive event such as the New Year, but you can purchase packaged *mochi* at grocery stores. There are electric *mochi* cookers too.

訳 餅は粘りの強い短粒米、もち米をついて塊にしたものです。餅アイスクリームは世界中で人気を集めていますが、これは最近作られた商品です。伝統的には餅は正月などの祝いの機会に手でつくものですが、餅のパックは食材店で購入できます。電気餅つき機もあります。

- □ rice cake　餅
- □ pound
  - 動（もちを）つく
- □ packaged
  - 形 パッケージ化された
- □ grocery　名 食料品

2 Some of the favorite classic *mochi* recipes are *isobemaki* (toasted, dipped in soy sauce and wrapped in crispy *nori* seaweed) and *kinako mochi* (dusted with toasted soybean flour and sugar).

訳 人気の餅のレシピには、磯辺巻き（焼いて醤油につけパリッとした海苔に巻く）、きなこもち（炒って粉にした大豆と砂糖にまぶす）などがあります。

- □ toast　動 焼く
- □ crispy
  - 形 パリッとした

3 *Mochi* is also used to make delicious sweets. For example, *ohagi* is *mochi* coated with sweet *adzuki* bean paste called *anko*.

訳 餅は美味しいお菓子にも使われます。例えばおはぎは餅をあんこという甘い小豆のペーストに包んだものです。

- □ be coated with
  - ～に包まれた
- □ paste　名 ペースト

45

 米
Rice

 125kcal | ¥〜1,000

メニュー **09** # カレーライス
Kare raisu / Japanese Curry

photo：Table-K / PIXTA (ピクスタ)

料理のキーワード

 食材
rice（米）, onion（玉ねぎ）, potato（じゃがいも）, carrot（人参）, meat（肉）, curry sauce（カレールー）wheat flour（小麦粉）, spice（香辛料）, cultet（カツ）, udon noodles（うどん）

調理法
simmer（煮込む）, thicken with（とろみをつける）, place on top of（〜の上にのせる）

 味わい
spicy（辛い）

説明してみよう！

20

1 Curry rice is one of the most popular dishes in Japan. Japanese curry is different from Indian curry. Indian curry is thin and eaten with long-grain rice, whereas Japanese curry is thickened with wheat flour and eaten with sticky short grain rice.

□thin 形 薄い
□thicken with
　〜でとろみをつける

訳 カレーライスは日本で最も人気の高い料理の一つ。日本のカレーはインドカレーと異なります。インドカレーはサラリとしていて長粒米とともに食べますが、日本のカレーは小麦粉でとろみをつけ、粘りのある短粒米とともに食べます。

2 The main ingredients are spices, onion, potatoes, carrots and other animal protein. *Katsu* curry is a pork cutlet placed on top of curry rice. Curry *udon* is *udon* noodles topped with Japanese curry sauce.

□animal protein
　動物性タンパク
□placed on
　〜にのせる

訳 主な材料はスパイス、玉ねぎ、ジャガイモ、ニンジンと動物性タンパクです。カツカレーはとんかつをカレーライスの上にのせたもの。カレーうどんはうどんの麺にカレーをかけたものです。

3 When people cook curry at home, it is common to use an instant sauce. You can find a whole variety of instant curry products at supermarkets. There are classic *yoshoku* restaurants that serve curry and curry-themed chain shops all over Japan.

□common
　形 一般的な
□instant 形 即席の
□chain shops
　チェーン店

訳 カレーを家で作る場合には、インスタントのソースを使うのが一般的です。多彩なカレーがスーパーに並んでいます。カレーを出す古典的な洋食 (p.188,189) レストランも、カレーをテーマにしたチェーン店も全国に存在します。

日本の麺料理
Japanese Noodles

日本人にとって麺料理は米同様に、重要な日常食です。日本の麺の独特な食べ方やその意味するところ、そして地域によって異なる麺の文化を紹介してみましょう。

photo：freeangle / PIXTA (ピクスタ)

麺—Facts

- 初のインスタントラーメン発売年 (the released year of the 1st instant *ramen*)
  —1958年 (1958)
- 日本でよく食べられている麺 (most eaten noodles in Japan)
  —①うどん (*Udon*) ②ラーメン (*Ramen*) ③そば (*Soba*)

参照：2018 年農林水産省データ

① Another staple of Japan
もう一つの日本の主食

21

The Japanese eat *soba*, *udon* and other types of noodles on a daily basis. There are many restaurants that specialize in noodles, but they can be fast food too.

 日本人はそば、うどんやその他の種類の麺料理を日常的に食べています。麺料理の専門店は数多に存在しますが、麺はファストフードでもあります。

For example, you can often find a *soba* eatery at a train station where you buy a ticket from the vending machine and eat a quickly served dish at a standing counter.

 例えば駅の構内で、自動販売機でチケットを買い、立ち食いカウンターでさっと出された料理を食べる蕎麦屋をよく見かけます。

- □ on a daily basis
  日常的に
- □ specialize in
  〜に特化する

- □ eatery 名 飲食店
- □ vending machine
  自動販売機
- □ standing counter
  立ち食いカウンター

② Eat fast and slurp
早くすすって食べよう！

It is crucial to eat Japanese noodles fast in order to fully enjoy its *koshi* (chewy "al dente" texture) before they get soggy. That is why you are encouraged to slurp loudly when you eat noodles in Japan. Slurping helps noodles to cool down with the air in your mouth.

☐ crucial	形 重要な
☐ chewy	形 噛み応えのある
☐ texture	名 食感
☐ soggy	形 ふやける
☐ encourage	動 勧める
☐ slurp	動 音を立てて食べる

訳 麺がのびてしまう前に、コシ（噛みごたえのある「アルデンテ」の食感）をしっかり楽しむため、日本の麺類は早く食べることがとても重要です。ずるずると大きな音を立てて食べるよう勧められるのはそのためです。音を立てることで、口の中の空気が麺の温度を下げてくれるのです。

③ The Regional Variations
地域性

They say people in the western part of Japan, such as Osaka, prefer *udon* served in a *kombu*-based, light-colored soup, whereas in the eastern part of Japan, including Tokyo, people like *soba* in a bonito-based, dark-colored soup. It is fun to compare such regional differences when you visit different cities in Japan.

☐ compare	動 比べる
☐ regional	形 地域の

訳 大阪など西の地方では、昆布をベースにした淡い色のつゆのうどんが好まれ、東京など東の地方では、鰹節をベースにした色の濃いつゆのそばが好まれると言われます。異なる都市を訪れる際に、地域による多様性を比べてみると楽しいものです。

スーパーでも、自宅での調理用（to cook at home）に様々な種類の生麺、乾麺を購入する（purchase various types of fresh and dried noodles）こともできます！

日本の麺料理
Japanese Noodles

🍚 60kcal　👛 ¥〜1,000

メニュー
10

ラーメン
Ramen / Ramen

photo：BASICO / PIXTA（ピクスタ）

料理のキーワード

🫑 食材　ramen noodles（中華麺）, soup（スープ）: *miso*, soy sauce, salt, pork born（豚骨）, *kombu*（昆布）, herb（香草）, topping（具）: *nori* seaweed（海苔）, egg（卵）, roasted pork（チャーシュー）, bamboo shoot（メンマ）

😊 味わい　*miso, tonkotsu*: thick（こってり）/ salt, soy sauce: thin（さっぱり）

説明してみよう！

1 Despite the origin from China, *ramen* is now a most representative dish of Japan. There are three components of *ramen*. Soup is made with *dashi* and seasonings like soy sauce and *miso*. Cooks develop their own recipes for their soup by combining multiple ingredients, such as pork bones, *kombu* and herbs.

□ component
　名 要素
□ develop
　動 開発する
□ combine
　動 混ぜ合わせる

訳 中国を起源にしながら、ラーメンは今や日本を代表する料理です。ラーメンは三つの要素から成っています。スープは出汁と醤油や味噌などの調味料を合わせたもの。料理人は豚骨、昆布、香草などのような多数の素材を合わせ、独自のスープレシピを開発します。

Two other components are toppings and noodles. These vary depending on the *ramen* shop and the region it is produced. Noodles can be thicker or thinner, and toppings reflect the local food culture.

□ vary　動 異なる
□ depending on
　〜による
□ reflect　動 反映する

訳 あとの二つの要素は具と麺。これらは店や地域により異なります。麺は太かったり細かったり、また具は地元の食文化を反映します。

2 The classic flavors are *miso*, salt, soy sauce and *tonkotsu* (pork bone-based thick soup). *Ramen* is regionally diverse. For instance, *tonkotsu* is popular in the south, whereas soy sauce-based *ramen* is common in Tokyo.

□ diverse　形 多様な

訳 代表的な味は味噌、塩、醤油と豚骨（豚骨をベースにしたこってりしたスープ）です。ラーメンは地域性が高い料理です。例えば豚骨は南に多いですし、東京では醤油ベースのラーメンが目立ちます。

主食
②

日本の麺料理
Japanese Noodles

様々なスタイルのラーメン
Various Styles of *Ramen*

photo：kuro3 / PIXTA（ピクスタ）

料理のキーワード

 食材

ramen noodles（中華麺）/instant ramen（インスタントラーメン）, soup（スープ）/dipping sauce（つけ汁）/ sliced omelet（錦糸玉子）, ham（ハム）, cucumber（きゅうり）, vinegar（酢）, sesame oil（ごま油）, soy sauce（しょうゆ）

 調理法

boil（ゆでる）, chill（冷やす）, slice（切る） top with（盛る）, dip into（浸ける）

52

1 Not all *ramen* come in a large bowl filled with soup. *Tsukemen* is noodles served with a dipping sauce. Noodles are quickly chilled after boiled to maximize the chewy texture.

訳▶すべてのラーメンがスープたっぷりの大きな器に出てくるわけではありません。つけ麺はつけ汁とともに出されるものです。麺は茹でたあとさっと冷やすのでコシがしっかり生かされます。

□chill 動 冷やす

2 Another type of *ramen* that is particularly popular in summer is *hiyashi chuka*. It is a soupless chilled *ramen* made with colorful toppings of thinly sliced omelet, ham and cucumber. It is flavored with a sauce made with vinegar, soy and sesame oil.

訳▶夏にことさら人気が高いのが冷やし中華です。スープなしの冷やしたラーメンで、薄く切った卵焼き、ハム、きゅうりといったカラフルな具が盛り込まれています。酢、醤油、ごま油を合わせたソースで味付けされています。

□particularly
副 特に
□soupless
スープのない
□cucumber
名 キュウリ
□flavor with
〜に味をつける

3 You can also enjoy *ramen* at home by buying instant *ramen* at supermarkets. You will be surprised by the quality and details put in them.

訳▶スーパーでインスタントラーメンを買って自宅で楽しむこともできます。食べてみると、その質の高さと入念さには驚かされます。

□quality 名 質
□detail
名 細部、入念さ

 165kcal | ¥～1,000

焼きそば
Yakisoba / Stir-fry Noodles

photo：Rhetorica / PIXTA (ピクスタ)

料理のキーワード

 食材

wheat noodles (小麦粉麺), pork (豚肉), onion (玉ねぎ), cabbage (キャベツ), Japanese green onion (ねぎ), bamboo shoot (竹の子), bean sprout (もやし), Worcestershire sauce (ウスターソース), oyster sauce (オイスターソース), *nori* seaweed flakes (青のり), red pickled ginger (紅生姜), bonito flakes (鰹節)

 調理法

stir-fry (炒める)

調理器具・器

hot iron plate (鉄板)

1 *Yakisoba* is a stir-fry dish made with wheat noodles similar to *ramen*. It is a popular dish at home as well as casual eateries including convenience stores. You may also find *yakisoba* being cooked on a big hot iron plate at a street festival called ennichi.

訳 焼きそばは、ラーメンに似た小麦粉の麺で作る炒め物です。家庭でもコンビニを含むカジュアルな飲食店でも人気の料理です。縁日と呼ばれるお祭りでも、大きな鉄板で焼かれている焼きそばを目にすることもあるでしょう。

□ stir-fry 名 炒め物
□ casual
　形 カジュアルな
□ eatery
　名 (簡易な) 飲食店
□ hot iron plate
　鉄板
□ street festival
　縁日
□ find ～ ing
　～しているのを目にする

2 Toppings of *yakisoba* vary depending on the region to reflect local food culture. Pork and vegetables, such as onion, cabbage, *negi* (Japanese green onion), bamboo shoots and bean sprouts, are the classic ones.

訳 焼きそばの具は地元の食文化を反映し様々です。豚肉と玉ねぎ、キャベツ、ネギ、たけのこ、もやしなどの野菜は代表的な具材です。

□ bamboo shoot
　たけのこ
□ bean sprout
　もやし

3 *Yakisoba* is flavored typically with a mixture of Worcestershire sauce, oyster sauce and soy sauce. The taste is full of *umami* (savory). The common *yakumi* garnish includes *nori* seaweed flakes, red pickled ginger and bonito flakes.

訳 焼きそばはウスターソース、オイスターソース、醤油を合わせたソースで味付けをしていることが多いです。その味は旨味たっぷりです。一般的な薬味は粉末のり、紅生姜、鰹節などです。

□ Worcestershire
　sauce
　ウスターソース
□ seaweed flakes
　青のり
□ bonito flakes
　鰹節

130kcal　¥〜1,000

メニュー
13

そば
Soba / Buckwheat Noodles

photo：jazzman / PIXTA（ピクスタ）

料理のキーワード

 食材　buckwheat flour（ソバ粉）, wheat flour（小麦粉）, dipping sauce（つゆ）, tempura（天ぷら）, egg（卵）, wild vegetable（山菜）

 調理法　boil（茹でる）, cool（冷やす）

 調理器具・器　bowl（丼）, woven bamboo tray（ざる）

 味わい　delicate（繊細な）

1 Buckwheat (*soba*) came to Japan from China in the 8th century. Since then the Japanese developed the technique to process buckwheat flour into noodles. The noodles are also called *soba*.

□ buckwheat
　名 ソバ
□ process… into ~
　…を~に加工する

訳 ソバの植物は8世紀に日本に伝来しました。以来そば粉を加工し麺にする技術が日本で発達しました。麺もそばと呼ばれます。

Soba is made with buckwheat flour and water, but normally wheat flour is added. Otherwise, gluten-free buckwheat is too brittle to keep the dough together. *Soba* is a healthy food. It is rich in vitamin B, rutin and fiber.

□ otherwise
　さもなければ
□ brittle
　形 こわれやすい
□ dough　名 生地
□ rutin　名 ルチン
□ fiber　名 食物繊維

訳 蕎麦は蕎麦粉と水で作りますが、通常小麦粉も加えます。そうしないと、グルテンを含まない蕎麦粉はもろすぎて生地にするのがとても難しいのです。蕎麦は健康食品です。ビタミンBやルチン、食物繊維を豊富に含んでいます。

2 *Soba* has a unique and delicate flavor. It can be enjoyed hot or cold. *Kake soba* is a bowl of *soba* in a soy sauce-based hot soup. *Mori soba* is boiled and cooled noodles served with soy sauce-based dipping sauce called tsuyu.

□ cooled　冷ました

訳 そばは独特な繊細な香りを持っています。熱くても冷たくても楽しめます。掛けそばは醤油ベースのスープに麺を入れた熱いそば料理。盛りそばは麺を茹でて冷やし、醤油ベースのつゆと呼ばれるつけ汁を添えたもの。

105kcal ￥～1,000

メニュー
14

うどん

Udon / Thick Japanese Noodles

photo：hattori / PIXTA（ピクスタ）

料理のキーワード

 食材
wheat flour noodles（小麦粉の麺）, soup（つゆ）, deep-fried *tofu* skin（油揚げ）, poached egg（温泉卵）, rice cake（餅）

 調理法
knead（こねる）, flatten（平たくする）, cut（切る）, roll（巻く）, top with（載せる）

 味わい
springy（弾力のある）/ soft（柔らかい）, smooth（するりとした）

説明してみよう！

1 *Udon* is thick noodles made with wheat flour served in a soy-based soup. There are a wide variety of toppings. The classic dishes include *kitsune udon* (topped with *abura age* or deep-fried *tofu* skin), *tsukimi udon* (poached egg) and *chikara udon* (*mochi*).

□ thick 形 太い
□ served in
　〜で提供する

訳 うどんは小麦粉で作った太い麺で、醤油ベースのスープと一緒に食べます。具材は多彩です。伝統的なものには（油揚げを上に載せた）きつねうどん、月見うどん（温泉卵）、力うどん（餅）などがあります。

2 There are mainly two types of *udon* noodles. *Teuchi* is made by kneading the dough, flattening it and cutting it by knife. *Tenobe* is rolled with oil to make a long noodle. *Tenobe* is more springy and smoother than *teuchi*.

□ knead 動 こねる
□ flatten
　動 平たくする
□ roll
　動 めん棒で生地を延ばす
□ springy
　形 弾力のある
□ smooth
　形 なめらかな

訳 うどんの麺には主に2種類あります。手打ちは生地をこね、平らにして包丁で切るものです。手延べは油を引きながら棒で生地を延ばし、一本の長い麺にします。手延べは手打ちより弾力があり、なめらかです。

3 *Udon* is regionally diverse, and each region boasts its own bowl of *udon*. *Kishimen* is similar to *udon* but it is wider and flatter, and has soft and smooth texture. It is popular in Nagoya.

□ boast 動 自慢する
□ flatter 形 平ら
□ smooth
　形 なめらか

訳 うどんは地域性が高く、各地方が独自のうどんを自慢にしています。きしめんはうどんに似ていますが、より幅が広く平らで、柔らかくするりとした食感があります。名古屋で一般的な料理です。

日本の麺料理
Japanese Noodles

 125kcal | 👛 ¥〜500

メニュー
15

そうめん
Somen / Thin Japanese Noodles

photo：marucyan / PIXTA（ピクスタ）

料理のキーワード

🫑 食材	wheat flour noodles（小麦粉の麺）, dipping sauce（つゆ）, Japanese green onion（ネギ）, *shiso* leaf（紫蘇）, ginger（生姜）, Japanese ginger（ミョウガ）
🔥 調理法	boil/ simmer（煮る）
😊 味わい	delicate（繊細な）, aromatic（香り高い）

説明してみよう！

1 *Somen* is a noodle dish that is popular in summer. *Somen* noodles are made of wheat flour. They are very thin (1.3mm or less in diameter) and delicate. *Somen* is normally served cold with a soy sauce-based dipping sauce called tsuyu.

☐ be made of
　〜でできている
☐ diameter 名 直径
☐ delicate 形 繊細な
☐ dipping sauce
　つけ汁

> **訳** そうめんは夏に人気の料理。そうめんの麺は小麦粉で作られています。麺はとても細く（1.3ミリ以下）繊細です。そうめんは通常、醤油ベースのつゆと呼ばれるつけ汁と一緒に冷やして出てきます。

Aromatic *yakumi* like Japanese green onion, *shiso*, ginger and *myoga* (Japanese ginger) are also served together. If the noodles are simmered in a hot soup, the dish is called *nyumen*.

☐ aromatic
　形 風味豊かな

> **訳** ねぎ、しそ、生姜、ミョウガなどの風味豊かな薬味も添えられています。麺が熱いスープに入っていた場合はにゅうめんと呼ばれます。

2 *Nagashi somen* is an entertaining way to eat *somen*. The noodles are put in water along a long bamboo gutter, and you catch them with your chopsticks. There are restaurants that feature *nagashi somen* in some cities. Some people install the bamboo gutter in their backyard for a fun party.

☐ entertaining
　形 楽しい
☐ gutter 名 水路、溝
☐ feature
　動 〜を呼び物にする
☐ install
　動 〜を設置する
☐ backyard 名 庭

> **訳** 流しそうめんは楽しいそうめんの食べ方。竹で作った水路の中に、水と一緒に入れた麺をお箸ですくって食べるものです。都市によっては流しそうめんを目玉にしたレストランが存在します。自宅の庭で竹の溝を設置して楽しいパーティーを開く場合もあります。

61

日本のパン
Japanese Breads

日本で発案されたパンは、海外の人にとっては驚きの連続かもしれません。コンビニやスーパーの商品を眺めながら紹介するのもいいですね。

photo：sunabesyou / PIXTA（ピクスタ）

パン—Facts

- パン消費量全国平均（average consumption of bread in Japan）
  — × 113/ 人（person）
- 本発祥パンの発売年（the released years of Japanese original breads）
  —あんパン（*an* bread）1874 年（1874）/ カレーパン（curry bread）1927 年（1927）

参照：総務省「家計調査 (2016 年)」

① The unique bread culture
独自のパン文化

⬇28

Bread was originally brought to Japan by the Portuguese in the 16th century, but it never became popular until sweet *an pan* (*pan* means bread)was invented by Kimuraya bakery in 1874.

□be brought to 〜にもたらされる
□Portuguese 名 ポルトガル人
□invent 動 開発する

訳 パンはもともと 16 世紀にポルトガル人が日本にもたらしたものですが、1874 年に木村屋が甘いあんぱん（「パン」は「パン」の意味）を開発するまでは、一般には普及しませんでした。

Savory bread became a staple in Japan after the World War II, when it became a part of school lunch menu. Since then more unique breads were invented, and now Japan boasts a bread culture of its own.

□savory bread 甘くない（惣菜）パン
□school lunch 給食
□boast 動 自慢する

訳 甘くないパン（惣菜パン）が日本の主食に加わったのは、給食でパンが出され始めた第二次世界大戦後です。以来個性的なパンがさらに生まれ、今や日本は独自のパン文化を誇ります。

② *Shoku pan* mirrors the Japanese palate
日本人の嗜好を反映する食パン

The Japanese like soft bread. Even crunchy baguettes are mostly softer than the original French version. *Shoku pan* is simple square bread used for toast and sandwiches. It is soft, fluffy, moist and slightly sweet. *Igirisu pan* (English bread) is a taller version of *shoku pan*, but it is crusty outside and chewy inside.

訳 日本人は柔らかいパンを好みます。カリッとしたバゲットですら、大半はフランス本来のものより柔らかく作られています。食パンはトーストやサンドイッチに使うシンプルなパン。ふわふわ柔らかく、しっとりとしてほのかな甘さを含んでいます。イギリスパンは食パンに似ていますが、高さがあり、表面がカリッとして中は噛みごたえがあります。

- ☐ crunchy
  形 カリカリした
- ☐ baguette
  名 バゲット
- ☐ fluffy　形 ふわふわの
- ☐ moist
  形 しっとりした
- ☐ slightly　副 わずかに
- ☐ crusty
  形 (表面が) 堅い
- ☐ chewy
  形 噛み応えのある

③ There are original Japanese sandwiches
日本独自のサンドイッチ

There is a variety of original Japanese sandwiches made with shoku pan. Examples are tamago (egg and mayo) and fruits (fruits and cream). You can also find a variety of creative sandwiches at convenience stores and supermarkets.

訳 食パンを使った日本ならではのサンドイッチもたくさんあります。玉子 (卵とマヨネーズ) やフルーツ (フルーツとクリーム) がその例ですが、創意あふれる多彩なサンドイッチがコンビニやスーパーに揃っています。

- ☐ creative
  形 独創的な

食パンとイギリスパンは、焼いてバターを塗るだけで (simply toast and butter)、その繊細さを楽しむことができます (you can enjoy the delicate taste of them)。

270kcal　¥～300

メニュー 16
菓子パン
Kashi pan / Sweet Pastries

photo：CORA / PIXTA (ピクスタ)

料理のキーワード

食材
pastry (パン菓子), bread (パン), *adzuki* bean paste (あんこ), sesame (ごま), poppy seeds (ケシのみ), salt-cured cherry petals (桜の塩漬け), custard (カスタード), chocolate cream (チョコクリーム)

調理法
fill with (詰める), garnish with (振りかける), shape (形をしている), steam (蒸す)

味わい
sweet (甘い), fluffy (ふわふわの), spongy (スポンジのような) silky (すべすべした), crusty (堅い表面の), rich (濃厚な)

説明してみよう！

1 Japanese sweet pastries are called *kashi pan*. They are classic western pastries incorporated with unique Japanese flavors. *Kashi pan* are so popular that you can find them everywhere including bakeries, supermarkets and convenience stores.

訳 日本風の甘いペーストリーを菓子パンと呼びます。伝統的な西洋のペーストリーに日本独自の風味を加えたものです。菓子パンはとても人気があるのでパン屋、スーパー、コンビニほかどこでも販売されています。

□pastry 名 パン菓子
□incorporate with ～と合体する

2 There are many types of *kashi pan*. *An pan* is a fluffy bread filled with red *adzuki* bean paste called *anko* and is often garnished with sesame, poppy seeds or salt-cured cherry petals.

訳 菓子パンには多くの種類があります。あんぱんは、ふわふわのパンにあんこと呼ばれる練り小豆を詰めたもので、ごま、ケシのみ、桜の花の塩漬けなどで飾りがついていることが多いです。

□fill with ～を詰める
□garnish with ～で飾る
□poppy seeds ケシの実
□salt-cured 塩漬けされた
□cherry petals 桜のはなびら

3 *Cream pan* is filled with silky custard. Melon pan features the shape and the pale green color of muskmelon with an addictive crusty mouth feel. *Korone* is shaped like the music instrument cornet filled with a rich chocolate cream.

訳 クリームパンはすべすべのカスタードを詰めたもの。メロンパンはマスクメロンの形と淡い緑色をかたどったもので、サクサクしたクセになる食感があります。コロネは楽器のコルネットの形で、濃厚なチョコレートクリームが入っています。

□silky 形 すべすべした
□custard 名 カスタード
□pale 形 淡い
□addictive 形 夢中にさせる
□crusty 形 （表面が）堅い
□mouth feel 名 口当たり
□music instrument 楽器
□rich 形 濃厚な

〜210kcal ¥〜300

惣菜パン
Sozai pan / Savory Breads

photo：Rain / PIXTA (ピクスタ)

料理のキーワード

 食材 bread (パン), **hot dog bun** (ホットドッグ用のパン), **curry** (カレー), **Japanese-style croquette** (コロッケ), **wiener sausage** (ウインナーソーセージ), **minced meat cutlet** (メンチカツ), ***yakisoba*** (焼きそば)

 調理法 **fry** (揚げる), **bake** (焼く), **fill with** (詰める)

 味わい **savory** (塩味のきいた)

1 Savory breads (*sozai pan*) are widely eaten in Japan as a snack or a meal. Curry *pan* is said to be the first savory bread developed in Japan around 1930. It is a fried or baked bread filled with Japanese curry.

□snack　名 おやつ
□be said to be
　〜と言われている

訳 惣菜パンはおやつや食事として幅広く食べられています。カレーパンは1930年頃、日本で最初に開発された惣菜パンと言われています。日本流のカレーを揚げた、もしくは焼いたパンに詰めたものです。

2 *Yakisoba* pan is *yakisoba* stuffed in a slit of a *koppe pan* like a hot dog. *Koppe pan* is similar to hot dog bun, but it is a nostalgic food for the Japanese, because it is a regular item at school lunches (and Japanese school lunches are delicious!)

□stuff in　〜に詰める
□slit　名 切り口
□hot dog bun
　ホットドッグ用のパンズ

訳 焼きそばパンはコッペパンを切って焼きそばをホットドッグのように挟んだものです。コッペパンはホットドッグのパンに似ていますが、日本の学校給食の定番品であることから、日本人にとって郷愁を誘うものです（そして日本の給食は美味しいのです！）。

3 Other popular fillings of savory breads include *korokke* (Japanese-style croquette), wiener sausage baked with ketchup and cheese or mayonnaise and *menchi katsu* (minced meat cutlet).

□filling　名 具
□wiener sausage
　ウインナー
□minced meat
　ひき肉

訳 他の惣菜パンの具には、コロッケ（日本流のパン粉を衣にした揚げ物）、ケチャップとチーズまたはマヨネーズと一緒に焼いたウィンナーソーセージ、メンチカツなどがあります。

日本の肉料理
Japanese Meat Dishes

世界にほこる和牛や、家庭や居酒屋の多彩な定番メニューを紹介しましょう。肉食禁止の歴史を話したら、色々なリアクションがかえってきそうですね。

photo：Job Design Photography / PIXTA（ピクスタ）

肉—Facts

- 肉消費量全国平均（annual average consumption of meat in Japan）— 33.2Kg/人（person）
- 最も食べられている肉（most eaten meats in Japan）—
  ①鶏肉（chicken）　②豚肉（pork）　③牛肉（beef）

参照：農林水産省「食肉鶏卵をめぐる情勢（2019年度）」

① The unique meat culture
独自の肉文化

31

Japan has an interesting relationship with meat. Since Buddhism arrived in Japan in the 6th century, eating meat was viewed as an unclean and unethical act of killing life. Especially, the nobles avoided eating meat.

□unclean	形 不潔な
□unethical	
形 倫理感に反する	
□noble	名 貴族
□avoid	動 避ける

 日本人は興味深い肉との関係を持っています。6世紀に仏教が伝来して以来、肉を食べることは不潔で、生き物を殺すという倫理観に反することとして見られていました。特に貴族は肉食を避けました。

In the late 19th century after Japan ended the political and commercial isolation of over 200 years, western diet suddenly became popular and the entire population started eating beef and other types of meat.

□commercial	
形 貿易上の	
□isolation	名 孤立
□diet	名 食事
□entire	形 全体の

 19世紀末、日本が200年以上に及ぶ、政治・貿易上孤立状態（鎖国）を解くと、西洋流の食事が一気に広まり、国民全体が牛肉や他の肉を食べるようになりました。

② *Wagyu*
和牛

Wagyu is a special type of meat the Japanese are proud of. It comes from four specific breeds of cattle that were the result of crossing of the Japanese native cattle with imported breeds. They are raised with special feeds and care, and the meat is highly marbled. The flavorful fat melts in your mouth.

- □ be proud of
  ～を誇りにする
- □ breed 名 品種
- □ cattle 名 畜牛
- □ native 形 在来の
- □ marbled
  形 霜降りの
- □ melt in
  ～の中で溶ける

 和牛は日本人が誇る特別な種類の肉。日本在来種と海外からの輸入種を掛け合わせて生まれた4品種の牛のことです。これらの牛は特別な飼料と世話を受けながら育ち、肉にはしっかりサシが入っています。風味豊かな脂肪は口の中で溶けます。

③ Kobe, *Wagyu* and *Washu*
神戸、和牛と和州牛

Kobe beef is famous outside Japan. It is a brand of *wagyu* produced in the Hyogo Prefecture. *Washu* beef, on the other hand, is not wagyu. You may find "*wagyu*" at a reasonable price, but it can be *washu* beef, which is a crossbred of *wagyu* and the American Black Angus.

- □ brand 名 ブランド
- □ reasonable
  形 手ごろな
- □ crossbred
  形 雑種の

 神戸牛は海外で有名です。これは兵庫県産の和牛のブランド名です。一方和州牛は和牛ではありません。手ごろな価格の「和牛」を見かけることがあるかもしれませんが、それは和牛とアメリカ産ブラックアンガス種の掛け合わせである和州牛かもしれません。

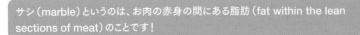

サシ (marble) というのは、お肉の赤身の間にある脂肪 (fat within the lean sections of meat) のことです！

🍚 310kcal | 👛 ¥～1,000

メニュー
18

唐揚げ
Karaage / Crispy Deep-fried Dish

photo:オクケン / PIXTA（ピクスタ）

料理のキーワード

| 食材 | batter（衣）, potato starch（片栗粉）, wheat flour（小麦粉）, chicken（鶏肉）, flounder（カレイ）, shrimp（エビ）, octopus（タコ）, burdock（ゴボウ）, glaze（タレ）, sesame seed（ゴマ） |

| 調理法 | deep-fried（揚げる）, marinate（漬けこむ）, brush with（〜を塗る）, sprinkle with（〜を散らす） |

| 味わい | crispy（カリっとした） |

説明してみよう！

32

1 *Karaage* is a crispy deep-fried dish. The thin batter is normally made with potato starch and wheat flour. The classic main ingredient is chicken. Other common ingredients include shrimp, octopus and *gobo* (burdock). *Karaage* is delicious either hot or cold. It is a popular dish at home, *izakaya* and for *bento* boxes.

訳 唐揚げはたっぷりの油でカリッと揚げた料理。通常片栗粉と小麦粉で作る薄い衣がついています。典型的な素材は鶏です。その他よく使われる食材はエビ、タコ、ゴボウなどです。唐揚げは熱くても冷めても美味しく食べられます。家庭でも居酒屋でもお弁当の具としても人気の料理です。

□ crispy
形 パリっとした
□ deep-fried
形 揚げた
□ batter 名 揚げ物の衣用の生地
□ starch 名 でんぷん
□ burdock 名 ゴボウ

2 There are regional *karaage* dishes too. *Tatsutaage* is one of them. Chicken or fish is marinated in soy sauce and *mirin* before fried. As a result, it has a darker color, which is said to resemble autumn leaves by the Tasuta River in Nara Prefecture.

訳 ご当地の唐揚げもあります。竜田揚げもその一つ。鶏や魚を醤油とみりんベースの漬け汁に漬けてから揚げるため、通常の唐揚げより濃い色で、それが奈良県の竜田川沿いの紅葉の色に似ているといわれます。

□ marinate
動 （タレに）漬け込む
□ resemble
動 〜に似ている
□ autumn leaves
紅葉

3 *Tebasaki* is another popular *karaage* particularly in Nagoya. Chicken wings are deep-fried, then brushed with a sweet glaze made with sugar and soy sauce and sprinkled with sesame seeds.

訳 手羽先は名古屋で特に人気の唐揚げ料理です。鶏の手羽先をたっぷりの油で揚げ、砂糖と醤油で作る甘いタレを塗り、ゴマを散らします。

□ chicken wings
手羽
□ brush with
〜を塗る
□ glaze 名 タレ
□ sprinkled with
〜を散らす

71

主菜① 日本の肉料理
Japanese Meat Dishes

340kcal | ¥～1,500

メニュー 19 トンカツ
Tonkatsu / Japanese-style Pork Cutlet

photo：ささざわ / PIXTA（ピクスタ）

料理のキーワード

食材
pork loin（豚ロース）, fillet（豚フィレ肉）, minced meat（ひき肉）, batter（衣）, wheat flour（小麦粉）, egg（卵）, bread crumbs（パン粉）, cabbage（キャベツ）, sauce made with vinegar, fruits, vegetables, and spices（トンカツソース）, Worcestershire sauce（ウスターソース）

調理法
deep-fried（揚げる）, slice（スライスする）, shred（千切りにする）

味わい
crispy（サクサクした）, light（軽い）, viscous（とろみのある）, sweet（あまい）

説明してみよう！

1 *Tonkatsu* is a Japanese-style pork loin or fillet cutlet. The crispy batter is made of wheat flour, egg and *panko*. *Panko* is lighter and larger breadcrumbs than western breadcrumbs.

訳 とんかつは和風の豚のロースまたはフィレのカツレツ。カリッとした衣は小麦粉、卵とパン粉でできています。パン粉は西洋のものより軽く粒が大きいパンのかけらです。

□ loin 名 ロース肉
□ fillet 名 ヒレ肉
□ breadcrumb 名 パン粉

2 Typically *tonkatsu* is sliced in bite-size pieces and served with *tonkatsu* sauce along with shredded cabbage. *Tonkatsu* sauce is made with vinegar, fruits, vegetables and spices. It is similar to, but more viscous and sweeter than Worcestershire sauce.

訳 通常とんかつは一口サイズに切って濃厚で甘いとんかつソースと千切りキャベツとともに盛られています。とんかつソースは酢、果物, 野菜と香辛料でできており、ウスターソースよりとろみがあります。

□ bite-size 一口サイズ
□ shredded 形 千切りにした
□ viscous 形 とろみのある
□ Worcestershire sauce ウスターソース

3 *Tonkatsu* is also served in different forms, such as on skewers (*kushikatsu*), sandwiches (*katsusando*), on top of Japanese curry (*katsu* curry) and on a bowl of rice cooked with onion, soy sauce and eggs (*katudon*). The minced meat version *menchikatsu* is popular too.

訳 とんかつには色々な形があります。串に刺した串カツ、サンドイッチにしたカツサンド、カレーにのせたカツサンド、玉ねぎ、醤油と卵と一緒にご飯にのせたカツ丼など。ひき肉を使ったメンチカツも人気の品です。

□ on skewer 串に刺した
□ minced meat ひき肉

73

主菜① 日本の肉料理
Japanese Meat Dishes

245kcal ¥〜1,000

メニュー
20
生姜焼き
Shoga Yaki / Ginger Grilled Pork

photo：ささざわ / PIXTA（ピクスタ）

料理のキーワード

🫑 食材	**thinly sliced pork loin**（薄切り豚ロース肉）, **onion**（たまねぎ）, **ginger**（ショウガ）
🔥 調理法	**grill**（焼く）, **marinate**（漬けこむ）, **brown**（きつね色に焼く）, **slice**（千切りにする）, **thicken**（とろみをつける）
😊 味わい	**refreshing**（さっぱりした）

74

1 Thinly sliced meat may not be very common in western countries, but it is very popular in Japan. *Shoga yaki* is a classic dish to feature thinly sliced pork. *Shoga* means ginger and *yaki* means grilled. *Shoga yaki* can be made with any ingredients, but it generally means a pork dish.

□feature
　動 主眼においた
□generally
　副 通常は

訳 肉の薄切りは西洋諸国ではあまり見かけませんが、日本ではとても人気があります。生姜焼きは薄切り豚肉をテーマにした典型的な料理です。生姜はジンジャー、焼きはグリルした料理を意味します。生姜焼きはどんな食材でも作ることができますが、通常は豚肉料理です。

2 Because of the thinness of the meat, it is quick and easy to make *shoga yaki*. Thinly sliced pork loin is marinated in ginger, soy sauce and *sake* for 10 minutes, and browned in a pan. Sliced onion may be also cooked together.

□thinness　名 薄さ
□marinate　動 漬ける
□brown
　動 きつね色に焼く

訳 肉が薄いことから、生姜焼きは簡単に作ることができます。薄切りにした豚のロースを生姜、醤油と日本酒に10分間漬け、フライパンで焼き色をつけます。玉ねぎのスライスと一緒に焼くこともあります。

3 To finish, a sauce made with soy sauce and sugar is added to the pan and cooked until the sauce thickens. The ginger makes the rich pork meat refreshing and delicious.

□thicken
　動 とろみをつける
□refreshing
　形 さっぱりした

訳 仕上げには、醤油と砂糖で作ったタレをフライパンに加え、ソースにとろみがつくまで火を入れます。豚の強い風味を生姜がさっぱり美味しくしてくれます。

75

200kcal | ¥〜1,000

メニュー
21
照り焼き
Teriyaki / Teriyaki

photo：Nutria / PIXTA（ピクスタ）

料理のキーワード

食材

chicken（鶏肉）, **yellowtail**（ハマチ）, **salmon**（サーモン）,
scallops（ホタテ貝）, *teriyaki* **sauce**（照り焼きソース）

調理法

pan-fry（フライパンで炒める）, **coat**（ソースをからめる）,
marinate（漬けこむ）,

味わい

sweet（あまい）, **salty**（しょっぱい）, **sheen**（照りのある）

説明してみよう！

1 *Teriyaki* is a versatile cooking method. It is often used in other countries too. Fish or meat is pan-fried and *teriyaki* sauce is added to the pan to coat the ingredient well.

訳 照り焼きは汎用性の高い調理法です。海外でもよく使われます。魚や肉をフライパンで焼き、照り焼きソースをフライパンに加えて食材にしっかりからめます。

□ versatile
形 汎用性の高い
□ pan-fried
フライパンでいためた
□ coat
動 (ソースを) からめる

2 *Teriyaki* sauce is made with soy sauce, *sake*, *mirin* and sugar. The sauce gives the beautiful amber color and sheen that stimulate your appetite. Also, the toasty, salty and sweet taste satisfies your palate.

訳 照り焼きソースは醤油、日本酒、みりんと砂糖で作ります。このソースは食欲を掻き立てる美しい琥珀色と照りを生み出します。また香ばしくしょっぱく甘い味わいは満足感を与えてくれます。

□ amber color
琥珀色
□ sheen 名 照り
□ stimulate
動 〜を刺激する
□ toasty 形 香ばしい
□ palate 名 味覚

3 Traditionally *teriyaki* is suitable for ingredients with firm and oily flesh such as chicken, yellowtail, salmon and scallops. But other recipes such as hamburger are popular nowadays.

訳 本来照り焼きは、鶏肉やハマチ、サーモンやホタテ貝などの身がしっかりとした脂の多い食材に適しています。しかし近年では、ハンバーガーなど他のレシピにも広く使われています。

□ firm
形 (身が) しっかりした
□ yellowtail
名 ハマチ
□ scallops
名 ホタテ貝

35

20~150kcal/本　¥~200

焼き鳥
Yakitori / Grilled Chicken on Skewers

photo：kai / PIXTA（ピクスタ）

料理のキーワード

 食材

chicken（鶏肉）, **pork**（豚肉）, **beef**（牛肉）, **thigh**（モモ）, **breast**（ムネ）, **tender breast**（ササミ）, **neck**（せせり）, **skin**（皮）, **wings**（手羽）, **heart**（ハツ）, **gizzard**（砂肝）, **liver**（レバー）, **tail**（ぼんじり）, **cartilage**（軟骨）, **Japanese green onion**（ねぎま）, **meatball**（つくね）

 調理法

grill over charcoal（炭火で焼く）/ **stove**（ガスで火入れする）

36

1 *Yakitori* means grilled chicken, but ingredients can be pork, beef or other meats.　The most popular type of *yakitori* is chicken on skewers grilled over charcoal or stove.　These are flavored with salt or *yakitori* sauce made with soy sauce, *mirin* and sugar.

□skewer　名 串
□charcoal　名 炭

訳 ▶ 焼き鳥は焼いた鳥という意味ですが、食材は豚、牛や他の肉にもなり得ます。最も一般的なのは炭火やガスで火入れした串焼きです。これらは塩または、醤油とみりんと砂糖で作る焼き鳥のタレで味付けされています。

2 *Yakitori* exemplifies the idea of *ichibutsu zentai*, because literally every part of chicken is on the menu. You will be surprised to discover deliciousness of these unknown parts of chicken.

□exemplify
副 例証する

訳 ▶ 焼き鳥は一物全体の考えを体現した料理。文字通りメニューには鶏の全ての部位が並んでいます。そんな未知の部位の美味しさには驚かされるはずです。

3 You can find *yakitori* at *izakaya* and other restaurants, but *yakitori ya* (*yakitori*-themed restaurant) is a great place to fully enjoy the charm of *yakitori*.

□charm　名 魅力

訳 ▶ 焼き鳥は居酒屋や他の飲食店でも食べられますが、その魅力を満喫するには焼鳥屋と呼ばれる専門店がいいでしょう。

🍚 225kcal | 👛 ¥〜1,500

 メニュー 23

角煮
Kakuni / Braised Pork Belly

photo：rogue / PIXTA（ピクスタ）

料理のキーワード

 食材

pork belly（豚のバラ肉）, braising liquid（煮汁）, herb（香草）, ginger（ショウガ）, Japanese green onion（ネギ）, boiled egg（ゆで卵）, *daikon* radish（大根）, Japanese *karashi* mustard（からし）

 調理法

braise（密閉した鍋で煮込む）, render out the excess fat（余分な脂肪を除く）

 味わい

fatty（脂ののった）, melting mouth feel（とろける食感）, rich（濃厚な）, sweet（甘い）

説明してみよう！

1 *Kakuni* is translated as "simmered square". It normally means braised pork belly. Cut the fatty layers of pork belly into large cubes and cooked them for hours until the excess fat is rendered out.

□braised　煮込んだ
□pork belly
　名 ブタのバラ肉
□cube　名 立方体
□excess　形 余分な
□render out
　～を除いた状態にする

> **訳** 角煮は「四角の煮物」を意味します。しかし通常豚のバラ肉の煮込みを指します。脂の入った豚の三枚肉を大きめの立方体に切り、余分な脂肪分が抜けるまで数時間煮込みます。

The melting mouth feel and the rich sweet taste along with the shiny caramel color make kakuni one of the most popular pork dishes in Japan.

□melting　形 溶ける
□mouth feel
　口当たり

> **訳** その口溶け感とカラメル色に輝く色合いと濃厚な甘みから、角煮は豚の最も人気料理の一つです。

2 The ingredients of the braising liquid of kakuni are soy sauce, *mirin*, *sake*, sugar. Herbs such as ginger and Japanese green onion are also added to lighten the smell of pork. Also, it is common to cook *daikon* radish or boiled eggs together in the pot, which absorbs the delicious flavor of the liquid. *Kakuni* is served with spicy Japanese mustard *karashi*.

□braising liquid
　煮汁
□lighten　動 和らげる

> **訳** 角煮の煮汁は醤油、みりん、日本酒と砂糖で作ります。生姜やねぎなどの香草も入れて豚の臭みを和らげます。また煮汁の美味しさをたっぷり吸収する大根やゆで卵を鍋に入れ、一緒に調理するのも一般的です。角煮には辛味の強い和がらし（日本のマスタード）を添えて出されます。

81

175kcal | ¥～1,500

メニュー
24

もつ料理
Motsu ryori / Organ Meats

photo：ささざわ / PIXTA（ピクスタ）

料理のキーワード

 食材

organ meat（内臓肉）, beef（牛肉）, pork（豚肉）, small intestines（小腸）, large intestines（大腸）, carrot（人参）, *daikon* radish（大根）, *tofu*（豆腐）, *konnyaku* root cake（こんにゃく）, Japanese green onion（ネギ）, ginger（ショウガ）,

 調理法

asimmer（煮込む）, bake on griddle（鉄板焼き）, bake on grill net over flame（直火網焼き）

 調理器具・器

hot pot（鍋）

1 *Motsu* means organ meats of animals. The Japanese like *motsu*, reflecting the philosophies of *ichibutsu zentai* and *mottainai*. Also, *motsu* are rich in vitamins, minerals and protein.

□organ 名 内臓
□philosophy 名 哲学

訳 もつとは動物の内臓肉のことです。日本人は一物全体やもったいないの理念を反映し、内臓肉を好みます。またもつは、ビタミン、ミネラル、タンパク質が豊富です。

There are a variety of ways to cook them deliciously. For example, simmered *motsu* is typically made with beef or pork's small or large intestines, carrots, *daikon* radish , *tofu* and *konnyaku* (a jelly-like root vegetable cake), ginger in a soy sauce or *miso*-based soup, and served with refreshing sliced Japanese green onion.

□intestine 名 腸
□cake 名 固めたもの
□root vegetable 根菜

訳 もつには美味しい食べ方がたくさんあります。例えばもつ煮は通常、牛か豚の小腸か大腸、人参、大根、豆腐、こんにゃく（ゼリーのような根菜を固めたもの）、生姜を醤油か味噌ベースの煮汁で煮込んだもので、さっぱりとしたねぎと一緒に出されます。

2 *Horumon yaki* is *motsu* baked on a griddle or on a grill net over a flame. *Motsunabe* is a hot pot made with *motsu*. There are many restaurants specialized in *motsu* dishes. Some areas such as Hakata in Fukuoka Prefecture are famous for them.

□griddle 名 鉄板
□grill net グリル網
□over a flame 直火で
□specialize in 〜を専門にする

訳 ホルモン焼きはもつを鉄板焼きか直火で網焼きにしたもの。もつ鍋はもつの鍋料理です。もつ料理専門店は多く存在します。福岡県の博多など、もつ料理で知られる地域もあります。

主菜②

日本の魚料理
Japanese Fish Dishes

定番料理はもちろん、世界最大の魚市場の活気や、
縁起がいいといわれる「出世魚」という言葉からも、
和食に欠かせない魚の魅力を紹介してみましょう。

photo：あんみつ姫 / PIXTA（ピクスタ）

魚—Facts

- 日本で最も食べられている魚（most consumed fish in Japan）—
  1. サケ（salmon）　2. マグロ（tuna）　3. ブリ（yellowtail）
- 漁獲量の多い3県（top 3 pref. of the largest catch in fishery）—
  1. 北海道（Hokkaido）　2. 長崎県（Nagasaki）　3. 茨城県（Ibaraki）

※総務省「家計調査」（平成 29 年）　※農林水産省「漁業・養殖業生産統計」（平成 28 年）

① The world's biggest fish market
世界最大の魚市場

39

Seafood is an essential part of *washoku*. There are over 500 species of edible fish around Japan. Also, the world's largest fish market exists in Tokyo.

 魚は和食の重要な一部です。日本近海には1000種も存在し、そのうち500種は食用です。また世界最大の魚市場は東京にあります。

- [ ] essential
  形 重要な
- [ ] edible　形 食用の

The Tsukiji Market opened in 1935, and became the space for over a thousand vendors trading the freshest seafood from all over the world. In October 2018, the market relocated to the new facility and renamed as the Toyosu Market.

 築地市場は1935年に開場し、1,000以上の業者が世界中から集まる魚介を取引する場となりました。2018年10月には新たな施設に移転し豊洲市場という名に変わりました。

- [ ] vendor　名 業者
- [ ] trade　動 取引する
- [ ] relocate
  動 移転する
- [ ] facility　名 施設
- [ ] rename as
  〜に名前を変える

② Invention of unique seafood dishes
独自の魚料理の創造

The ample supply of fish in Japan led to invention of a number of unique seafood dishes. For example, *nigiri zushi* was born as casual fast food in the 19th century. Street vendors in Tokyo used to sell vinegared rice with fresh raw fish that came from the nearby Tokyo Bay.

- □ample 形 豊富な
- □invention 名 開発
- □casual 形 創案
- □street vendor 路上の屋台業者
- □used to かつては～
- □raw 形 生の

 訳 日本の豊富な魚の供給は、たくさんの独自の魚料理の創造をもたらしました。例えば握り鮨は、19世紀にカジュアルなファストフードとして生まれたものです。東京の屋台では東京湾付近でとれた新鮮な生魚を酢飯にのせて大衆に売っていました。

③ The evolution of a name
進化する名称

The name of Japanese fish sometimes changes over their lifetime to reflect the size and its market value. They are called *shusse uo*. For instance, *wakashi* is baby yellowtail, which becomes *inada*, *warasa* and finally *buri*. Since the name change could connote advancement to the next level in life, they are often served at festive occasions.

- □change over 切り替わる
- □lifetime 名 生涯
- □reflect 動 反映する
- □market value 市場価値
- □yellowtail 名 ブリ
- □connote 動 意味を含む
- □advancement 名 前進

訳 日本の魚の中には、その大きさと市場価値を反映し、生涯を通じて呼称が変わるものがあります。それらは出世魚と呼ばれます。例えば幼いブリであるワカシはイナダ、ワラサ、そして最後にブリになります。改名は人生の次のレベルへの前進という意味合いも持つ為、こうした魚は祝いの席でよく出されます。

主菜②

日本の魚料理
Japanese Fish Dishes

サンマ **3100**kcal / サワラ**2000**kcal

メニュー
25

焼き魚
Yaki zakana / Grilled Fish

photo：ゴスペル / PIXTA（ピクスタ）

料理のキーワード

 食材

fish（魚）, mackerel（さわら）, sea bass（スズキ）, pacific
saury（サンマ）, yellowtail（ブリ）, white *miso*（白味噌）,
citrus（柑橘類）, marinade（マリネ）

 調理法

grill（焼く）, flavor with（〜で味付けする）

1 Grilled fish (*yaki zakana*) is very popular in Japan. It is a classic item of *ichju sansai* meal, and is often found on breakfast and lunch *teishoku* (set menus).

訳 焼き魚は日本で人気です。一汁三菜の代表的な料理で、朝食やランチ定食でも目立ちます。

Since fish is highly seasonal in Japan, it is a great way to enjoy various flavors of fish. For instance, look for mackerel in spring, sea bass in summer, pacific saury in fall and yellowtail in winter.

訳 魚は日本で季節性が高いので、焼き魚は多彩な魚の風味を味わうのにもってこいです。例えば春にはさわら、夏にはスズキ、秋にはサンマ、冬にはブリなどを探してみましょう。

2 There are many ways to make grilled fish. Fish can be flavored with salt, sweet white *miso* (*saikyo yaki*), sweet soy sauce (*teri yaki*) and soy sauce and citrus-based marinade (*yuan yaki*).

訳 焼き魚には様々な調理法があります。魚の味付けには塩、甘い白味噌（西京焼き）、甘い醤油のソース（照り焼き）、醤油と柑橘類の果汁のマリネ（幽庵焼き）などが使われます。

Robata yaki is an authentic style of cooking where you sit fireside and cook fish.

訳 炉端焼きは火の側に座って魚を焼く伝統料理です。

□ grilled fish　焼き魚

□ seasonal
　形 季節性の
□ mackerel　名 さわら
□ sea bass　スズキ
□ pacific saury
　サンマ

□ flavor with
　〜で味付けする
□ marinade
　名 マリネ
□ authentic
　形 れっきとした

主菜
②

日本の魚料理
Japanese Fish Dishes

カレイ **105**kcal / サバ **220**kcal

メニュー 26

煮付け
Nitsuke / Simmered Fish

photo：gontabunta / PIXTA（ピクスタ）

料理のキーワード

 食材
fish（魚）, flounder（カレイ）, sea bream（鯛）, mackerel（サバ）

 調理法
simmer（煮る）

 調理器具・器
pot（鍋）, drop-lid（落し蓋）

 味わい
umami（旨み）

88

1 Simmering is a popular cooking method in *washoku*. There are different types of simmered food, and *nitsuke* is typically used for fish.

□method 名 方法

訳 煮物は日本でよく使われる調理法です。煮物にはいくつも種類があり、魚には煮付けがよく使われます。

The liquid for simmering is made with soy sauce, *sake, mirin* and sugar. Fish is cooked in a pot with a small amount of the liquid that just covers the fish. A drop-lid covers the fish while it is being cooked, so that the fish absorbs the flavor of the liquid well.

□liquid 名 汁
□drop-lid 落とし蓋
□absorb 動 吸収する

訳 煮汁は醤油、酒、みりんと砂糖で作られています。魚がかぶるくらいの煮汁を鍋に入れて作ります。煮汁の風味がしっかり魚につくよう、調理中は落し蓋で魚に蓋をします。

2 Popular fish for *nitsuke* includes flounder, sea bream and mackerel.

□flounder 名 カレイ
□sea bream 鯛
□mackerel 名 サバ

訳 煮付け用の定番の魚には、カレイ、鯛、サバなどがあります。

Fish with strong flavor like mackerel is often cooked with *miso*, ginger, *sake*, soy sauce and sugar. This is called *miso-ni*. The flavor of *miso* reduces the fishiness as well as increases *umami*.

□fishiness 名 魚臭さ

訳 サバのように匂いの強い魚は、よく味噌、生姜、酒、醤油と砂糖と一緒に調理されます。これを味噌煮と言います。味噌の風味が魚臭さを和らげると同時にうま味を高めます。

主菜
②

日本の魚料理
Japanese Fish Dishes

アジ **120**kcal / イワシ **165**kcal

メニュー
27

南蛮漬け

Nanbanzuke / Karaage Marinated in Spicy Vinegar Sauce

photo：しまじろう / PIXTA（ピクスタ）

料理のキーワード

 食材
horse mackerel（アジ）, sardine（イワシ）, Japanese smelt（ワカサギ）, salmon（サーモン）, chicken（鶏肉）, herb（香草）, spice（香辛料）, vinegar（酢）, Japanese green onion（ネギ）,chili pepper（唐辛子）

 調理法
deep-fry（揚げる）, marinate（マリネに漬ける）

 味わい
richness（こってり感）, refreshing（さっぱりした）, spiciness（辛い）

1 *Nanban* means "southern barbarians". The origin of the term is the arrival of the Portuguese and the Spanish in Japan in the 16th and 17th centuries. Deep-frying and the use of herbs and spices were some of the things the *nanban* people brought to Japan.

> 訳 南蛮とは「南の野蛮人」を意味します。この言葉の由来は、16、17世紀に東南アジア経由で日本にやってきたポルトガル人とスペイン人です。たっぷりの油で揚げることや、香草やスパイスの使用は、彼らが日本に伝播したものの数例です。

That is why *nanbanzuke* is the dish of *karaage* marinated in a sauce that is made with vinegar, Japanese green onion, chili pepper, soy sauce and sugar. You can find a similar dish in Portugal and Spain called escabeche.

> 訳 なので酢、ねぎ、唐辛子、醤油と砂糖で作った漬け汁に漬けた唐揚げが、南蛮漬けと呼ばれるのです。ポルトガルやスペインには、エスカベシュという似た料理があります。

2 *Nanbanzuke* is prepared with various ingredients, such as horse mackerel, sardine, and chicken. The combination of the richness of deep-fry, the refreshing vinegar sauce and the spiciness of chili pepper makes *nanbanzuke* popular in Japan.

> 訳 南蛮漬けは、アジ、イワシ、鶏肉など様々な食材で作ります。たっぷりの油で揚げるこってり感と、さっぱりした酢の漬け汁、唐辛子の辛さの組み合わせにより、南蛮漬けは日本で人気を集めています。

□ barbarian
名 野蛮人
□ deep-fry 揚げる
□ herb 名 香草

□ prepare with
〜で料理する
□ horse mackerel
アジ
□ sardine 名 イワシ
□ combination
名 組みあわせ

91

エビ **195**kcal / アナゴ **240**kcal

メニュー
28

天ぷら
Tempura / Tempura

photo：midori_chan / PIXTA（ピクスタ）

料理のキーワード

 食材

batter（バッター液）, egg（卵）, wheat flour（小麦粉）, iced water（氷水）, dipping sauce（漬け汁）, shrimp（エビ）, conger eel（アナゴ）, sweet fish（アユ）, cod（タラ）, sand borer（キス）, white fish（白身魚）, vegetable（野菜）,

 調理法

deep-fry（揚げる）, chill（冷やす）

 味わい

light（軽い）, delicate（繊細な）, crispy（サクサクした）, airy（ふんわりとした）,

1 Compared to other types of deep-fried dishes, *tempura* is lighter and more delicate.   The batter is made with egg, wheat flour and iced water.

訳 大量の油で揚げた他の料理に比べ、天ぷらはより軽く繊細です。衣は卵、小麦粉と氷水。

□delicate 形 繊細な
□batter 名 衣

2 Perfectly made *tempura* is airy and maximizes the flavors of seasonal ingredients.   *Tempura* is served with a dipping sauce made with *dashi*, soy sauce and *mirin* or salt, depending on the type of seafood.

訳 完璧に揚がった天ぷらはふんわりとして、旬の食材の風味をフルに引き出しています。天ぷらは素材により、だし、醤油、みりんで作る漬け汁、もしくは塩とともに出されます。

□airy
　形 ふんわりとした

3 The best seafood for tempura includes shrimp, conger eel, cod, and other less fatty white fish to keep the dish not too rich.   That is why vegetables are also suitable for tempura.   There are expensive tempura restaurants where skilled chefs carefully fry food in front of you.

訳 味がくどくなりすぎないよう、天ぷらに最も適した食材はえび、アナゴ、タラやその他脂の少ない白身魚です。そのため野菜も天ぷらに向いています。高級天ぷら店に行くと、熟練シェフが丁寧に目の前で天ぷらを揚げてくれます。

□conger eel　アナゴ
□cod 名 タラ
□fatty 形 脂肪質の

日本の魚料理
Japanese Fish Dishes

🍚 215kcal | 👛 ¥3,000〜

メニュー 29

うなぎ丼
Unagi Don / Grilled Eel on Rice

photo：kai / PIXTA（ピクスタ）

料理のキーワード

 食材
eel filet（鰻の切り身）, rice（米）, *teriyaki* sauce（照り焼きソース）, *sansho* pepper（山椒）

 調理法
grill（焼く）, glaze with（〜で照りをつける）, sprinkle over（ふりかける））

 調理器具・器
bowl（丼）, box（お重）

 味わい
nutritious（栄養豊富な）

94

説明してみよう！

1 *Unagi don* or *unadon* is grilled eel filet on hot rice. It is glazed with a sauce similar to *teriyaki* sauce. When the eel is served in a box, the dish is called *una ju*.

訳 うなぎ丼、もしくはうな丼は、熱いご飯にのせた焼き鰻です。照り焼きソースに似たソースで照りが付いています。鰻を重箱に入れたものはうな重と呼ばれます。

□filet 名 切り身
□glaze with
　〜で照りをつける

Sansho pepper is sprinkled over the fish at the table, which is believed to help digestion.

訳 食べる直前に、消化を助けるとされる山椒を鰻にふりかけます。

□sprinkle
　動 振りかける
□digestion 名 消化

The dish was invented during the Edo period in Tokyo, but there are many restaurants specialized in *unagi* dishes all over the country.

訳 この料理は江戸時代に東京で生まれたものですが、日本中に多くの鰻料理店が存在します。

2 *Unagi* is highly nutritious. It is rich in A, B, D, E vitamins and omega-3 fatty acids. That is why there is a unique tradition of eating eel to boost energy on doyo no ushi no hi in mid-summer in Japan.

訳 鰻は栄養豊富です。ビタミンA, B, D, Eとオメガ3脂肪酸が多く含まれています。だから日本には、夏の盛りの土用の丑の日に鰻を食べて活力を増強するという独特の慣習があるのです。

□nutritious
　形 栄養豊富な
□boost
　動 〜を増強する

日本の魚料理
Japanese Fish Dishes

メニュー
30

刺身
Sashimi / Sashimi

photo：june. / PIXTA（ピクスタ）

料理のキーワード

 食材　seafood（魚介類）, fish（魚）

 調理法　cure with kombu（昆布締めする）, wash in ice water（冷水で洗う）, cut（切る）, dip in（漬ける）

 味わい　raw（生の）, *umami*（旨みのある）, thin（薄い）

96

説明してみよう！

 45

1 *Sashimi* is *sushi* minus rice. It represents the aesthetics of *washoku*. It is simple, yet takes a lot of work to make a perfect slice of raw seafood. For instance, fish is cured with *kombu* to add *umami*, or washed in ice water to make the texture better.

訳▶刺身は鮨から米を除いたものです。刺身は和食の美学を体現しています。刺身はシンプルながらも、完璧な一切れを生み出すのは大仕事です。例えば魚のうま味を増すために昆布締めにしたり、冷水で洗って食感を高めたりします。

- □ minus
  前 〜を引いた
- □ represent 動 表す
- □ aesthetics 名 美学
- □ cure with
  〜で保存処理する
- □ texture 名 食感

2 There are many special techniques to cut fish for *sashimi*. An example is *sogi giri*. It makes a thinner cut and a larger surface to enhance its taste and mouth feel of fish with firm texture.

訳▶刺身用に魚を切るにはいくつもの特別な技法があります。一例はそぎ切り。薄く、かつ断面を大きくする切り方で、身の締まった魚の味と食感を高めます。

- □ surface 名 表面
- □ enhance 動 高める
- □ firm
  形 身の締まった

3 When you eat *sashimi*, put a tiny piece wasabi on top of it and dip it in your soy sauce lightly, instead of melting wasabi in the soy sauce. In this way you will enjoy the flavor of the fish to the fullest.

訳▶刺身を食べる時には、山葵を醤油に溶かす代わりに、少量を刺身一切れにのせ、醤油に軽く漬けます。そうすれば魚の味を満喫できます。

- □ tiny 形 小さな
- □ dip 動 浸す
- □ melt 動 溶かす
- □ to the fullest
  最大限に

97

🍚 マグロ赤身 **125**kcal／ホタテ **70**kcal

メニュー
31

刺身の魚の種類
Types of Fish for *Sashimi*

photo：Sunrising / PIXTA（ピクスタ）

料理のキーワード

 食材

seafood（魚介類）, white meat fish（白身魚）, sand borer（キス）, needlefish（サヨリ）, sea bass（スズキ）, sea bream（タイ）, fluke（ヒラメ）, blowfish（フグ）, red meat fish（赤身魚）, tuna（マグロ）, skipjack tuna（カツオ）, blue fish（青魚）, horse mackerel（アジ）, mackerel（サバ）, sardine（イワシ）, pacific saury（サンマ）, shellfish（貝）, scallop（ホタテ）, ark shell（赤貝）, giant clam（ミル貝）, squid（イカ（甲なし））, cuttlefish（イカ（甲あり））, octopus（タコ）, salmon roe（いくら）, sea urchin（ウニ）, garnish（薬味）, *daikon* radish（大根）, ginger（ショウガ）

😊 **味わい**

light（さっぱり）, rich（こってり）

98

説明してみよう！

46

1 There are four types of seafood used for *sashimi*. White meat fish includes sand borer, sea bream, and blowfish. Red meat fish includes tuna and skipjack tuna. Blue fish is a type of red meat fish, but also has a bluish, shiny skin. Examples are horse mackerel, mackerel, sardine and pacific saury.

訳 刺身用の魚は4種類に分けられます。白身魚はキス、タイ、フグなど。赤身魚は マグロ、カツオなど。青魚は赤身魚ですが、青味がかった光沢のある皮を持った種類です。アジ、サバ、イワシ、秋刀魚がその例です。

Shellfish and other types include scallops, ark shell, giant clam, squid, octopus, salmon roe and sea urchin.

訳 貝やその他の種類にはホタテ、赤貝、みる貝、イカ、たこ、いくら、ウニなどがあります。

2 In order to enjoy the taste of *sashimi* fully, people normally eat in the order from light to rich: white meat fish or blue fish, shellfish and other types, red meat fish. They are served with decorative garnishes such as *daikon radish*, ginger, and *shiso*. These are all edible and help digestion as well as kill harmful bacteria.

訳 刺身を十分に味わうには、通常さっぱりしたものからこってりしたものの順で食べます。白身魚か青魚、貝やその他の種類、赤身魚の順です。これらは大根、生姜、しそなどの薬味で飾られて出てきます。薬味は全て食用で、消化を助け殺菌効果もあります。

□blowfish 名 フグ
□skipjack tuna カツオ
□bluish 形 青みがかった

□ark shell 赤貝
□giant clam ミル貝
□squid 名 イカ
□roe 名 魚卵
□sea urchin ウニ

□in order to ～するために
□in the order ～の順番で
□light 形 さっぱりした
□rich 形 こってりした
□decorative 形 飾られている
□edible 形 食用の
□digestion 名 消化
□bacteria 名 菌

珍しい魚の部位
Odd Parts of Seafood

海外では、フィレなどの魚の中心部だけ食べるのが一般的です。しかし日本では魚のすべての部位を味わいます。しかも変わった部位であるほど、より美味しく栄養価が高いことがあります。例えばエンガワはカレイなどの平たい魚の尾びれの筋肉から取れます。コリコリしてコラーゲンが豊富です。あん肝はアンコウの肝で、その濃厚さから海のフォアグラと呼ばれますが、より繊細でビタミンAが豊富です。外国人は日本人がタラ、ふぐ、あんこうなど雄魚の精巣を食べると知りよく驚きますが、柔らかくクリーミーで、蛋白質、ビタミン、ミネラルに富んでいます。カマは魚の頭とエラの後ろにある骨についた、柔らかく脂の多い首の部分です。

It is common to eat only the main parts of fish such as fillet abroad. But the Japanese appreciate every part of seafood. And the more unusual parts can be the more delicious and nutritious. For instance, *engawa* comes from the tail fin muscles of flatfish such as flounder. It is crunchy and rich in collagen. *Ankimo* is monkfish liver and often called foie gras of the sea for its richness, but it is more delicate and high in vitamin A. Foreigners are often surprised to find that the Japanese enjoy eating milt, or sperm sacs, of male fish such as cod, blowfish and monkfish, but it is soft and creamy, and full of protein, vitamins and minerals. *Kama* is fish collar, which is the tender fatty meat on the bone behind the head and gills.

会席
Kaiseki

最近海外の多くのトップシェフが、正式な伝統和食のコース料理である会席料理の要素を取り入れています。彼らは旬の素材の使用の重視や美しく盛り付けた小皿など、会席独自の特徴にひらめきを得ているのです。和の盛り付けは、西洋のように対称を強調せず個性的です。代わりに皿の片側に余分に空間を設けるなど、自然な形を重視します。

会席は江戸時代に生まれました。これは 15 世紀頃に武士が生み出した、形を重んじ特別な機会に供される本膳料理を簡素化したものです。ちなみに懐石は、茶席の前に出される質素な料理のことを意味します。

In recent years, many top chefs in the world use elements of *kaiseki*, a formal and traditional Japanese multi-course dinner. They are inspired by the unique characteristics of *kaiseki*, such as strong focus on seasonal ingredients and beautifully plated small dishes. The Japanese style of plating is unique, because unlike the western-style plating, chefs do not emphasize symmetry. Instead, they try to feature natural forms, such as leaving more space on one side of the plate.

Kaiseki was born in the Edo period. It is the simplified form of *honzen ryori*, which was developed by samurais around 15th century as a ritualistic meal served for formal occasions. *Kaiseki* also means a simple meal served before a tea ceremony.

副菜 Side dishes

副菜には手間をかけずに作れる品が定番です。シンプルながら、食卓の味、色、栄養を補完してくれる副菜について紹介してみましょう。

副菜—Facts

- 夕飯時の副菜の平均品数（average items of side dishes for dinner in Japan）—
  ① 2品（2 dishes）② 3品（3 dishes）③ 4品（4 dishes）
- 納豆の年間平均支出額（annual average natto consumption in Japan）—
  ¥4,000/世帯（householding）

参照：フジッコ株式会社 2012 年調べ / 総務省「家計調査 2016~2018 年平均」

① The *washoku* principle and side dishes
和食の原則と副菜

⬇️47

The basic *washoku* meal follows the principle of *ichiju sansai*. Therefore the cook needs to prepare one main dish and two other smaller dishes in addition to *miso* soup and rice at the table.

□follow 動 ～に従う
□principle 名 原則

訳 基本の和食の食事は一汁三菜の原則にならいます。そのため料理する人は、みそ汁とご飯に加え、主菜と2つの副菜を準備する必要があります。

These smaller dishes can be freshly cooked like the entree, but it is difficult to make so many items to fill the table at each meal. That is why *ichiju sansai* menus include items that do not require a lot of preparation.

□freshly 形 新鮮な
□entree 名 主菜
□preparation 名 準備

訳 副菜は主菜のようにつくりたてを出すこともできますが、毎食食卓を埋めるのは容易ではありません。そこで一汁三菜のメニューには、手間がかからない料理が含まれています。

② Classic menu items
定番メニュー

ou can often find simmered foods that can be served over a few meals. Easy items such as eggs, *tofu* and Japanese-style salads are popular too.

☐ simmered food
煮物

訳 数回の食事にわたって出すことのできる煮物は人気です。卵や豆腐、和風のサラダも定番です。

③ Try *teishoku*
副菜を体験できる場

 great way to experience an *ichiju sansai* meal is to eat *teishoku*. *Teishoku* means a set menu, which you can easily find at a hotel breakfast and many restaurants during lunchtime. There are normally a few choices of the main dish, and smaller dishes also come with it.

☐ experience
名 体験
☐ come with
〜に付いている

訳 一汁三菜の食事を体験するには定食がいいでしょう。定食とはセットメニューのことで、ホテルの朝食や昼時のレストランで容易に見つかります。たいていいくつか主菜の選択肢があり、そこに副菜も付いてきます。

These smaller dishes complement the main dish with taste, colors and nutrition. *Teishoku* is also a good meal for value-oriented eaters.

☐ oriented
形 〜志向の

訳 これらの副菜は主菜の味、色、栄養を補完します。定食はお値打ちを求める人にもおすすめです。

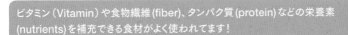
ビタミン（Vitamin）や食物繊維（fiber）、タンパク質（protein）などの栄養素（nutrients）を補充できる食材がよく使われてます！

副菜
Side dishes

出汁巻き玉子 **120**kcal / 茶碗蒸し **100**kcal

メニュー
34

たまご料理
Tamago ryori / Egg Dishes

photo：I / PIXTA（ピクスタ）

料理のキーワード

 食材　egg（卵）, custard,（カスタード）, shrimp（エビ）, fish cake（かまぼこ）, *shiitake* mushroom（しいたけ）, ginko nut（銀杏）, *mitsuba* leaf（みつば）/ silken *tofu*（玉子豆腐）/ raw egg（生卵）, rice（米）

 調理法　roll（巻く）, steam（蒸す）, chill（冷やす）, mix with（混ぜる）

 味わい　fluffy（ふわふわした）, smooth（なめらかな）

説明してみよう！

1 There are many unique dishes made with egg in Japan. For example, *dashimaki tamago* is a dashi -flavored omelet rolled carefully in a pan. They say it is a test of chefs' skills.

□roll 動 巻く

訳 日本には個性的なたまごがたくさんあります。例えば出汁巻き玉子は出汁で風味づけした卵を、フライパンで丁寧に巻かれたオムレツです。料理人の技量を図るテストと言われます。シンプルですが料理人の技量を反映する重要な料理です。

Chawan mushi is fluffy smooth custard made with egg and *dashi*. It is steamed with a variety of ingredients including shrimp, fish cake, *shiitake* mushroom, gingko nuts and *mitsuba* leaves.

□fluffy
形 ふわふわした
□custard
名 カスタード
□fish cake かまぼこ
□gingko nut 銀杏

訳 茶碗蒸しは、えび、かまぼこ、しいたけ、銀杏、みつばなどの多彩な素材とともに蒸して作る、ふわふわすべすべした卵と出汁のカスタードです。

Tamago dofu(*tofu*) is a silken tofu made with eggs and *dashi*. It is similar to the *chawanmushi* custard, but served chilled.

□silken
形 きめの細かき
□chilled 形 冷やした

訳 玉子豆腐は出汁と卵で作るきめの細かい豆腐です。茶碗蒸しのカスタードと似ていますが、これは冷やして提供します。

2 In Japan, it is common to eat raw eggs even for children. For instance, *tamagokake gohan* is a raw egg mixed with rice in a bowl flavored with soy sauce.

□raw 形 生の

訳 日本では子供でも生卵を食べるのが普通です。例えば卵かけご飯は、ご飯に生卵を混ぜ、醤油で味付けしたものです。

105

200kcal　¥～100

メニュー 35 納豆
Natto / Fermented Soybeans

photo：taa / PIXTA（ピクスタ）

料理のキーワード

 食材　soybean（大豆）, *karashi* mustard（からし）, Japanese green onion（ネギ）

 調理法　ferment（発酵させる）, top with（～をのせる）, stir（かき混ぜる）

 調理器具・器　chopsticks（箸）

 味わい　stringy (gooeyness)（ねばねばした）, distinctive smell（独特のにおい）, *umami*（旨みのある）

1 *Natto* is fermented soybeans with a uniquely stringy texture. It is often called a super food for its ample nutrients as well as the powerful enzyme called nattokinase. Many Japanese eat it every day for breakfast.

訳 納豆は独特の粘りを持つ、発酵させた大豆です。豊富な栄養素と、ナットウキナーゼという強力な酵素を持つことからスーパーフードとも呼ばれます。毎朝食べる日本人がたくさんいるほど人気の高いものです。

You can find a variety of *natto* brands at supermarkets made with small to large-sized beans and different flavorings.

訳 スーパーでは、大小様々なサイズの豆や異なる味付けの商品が並んでいます。

2 *Natto* has a distinctive smell. That is why some people don't like it. To lighten the smell, *natto* is typically topped with dashi-infused soy sauce, *karashi* mustard and green onion.

訳 納豆には独特の香りがあります。嫌いな人がいるのはそのためです。その香りを和らげるために、納豆には通常出汁風味の醤油、からしとねぎをのせます。

Natto is normally stirred with chopsticks many times before eaten. Stirring increases the gooeyness and the smell, but is also beleived to increase *umami*.

訳 納豆は普通何度も箸で混ぜてから食べます。そうすると粘りも匂いも強まりますが、うま味も増すと言われています。

□ **ferment**
動 発酵させる
□ **stringy**
形 粘りをもった
□ **super food**
スーパーフード（栄養価にすぐれていると言われる食品）
□ **nutrient** 名 栄養素
□ **enzyme** 名 酵素

□ **flavoring**
名 調味料

□ **distinctive**
形 独特の
□ **infused**
形 ～風味の

□ **stir with**
動 ～でかき混ぜる
□ **gooeyness**
名 粘り気

副菜
Side dishes

80kcal ¥～100

豆腐
Tofu / Coagulated Block of Soymilk

photo：Key West / PIXTA (ピクスタ)

料理のキーワード

 食材
soy milk (豆乳), ginger (ショウガ), bonito flakes (鰹節), Japanese green onion (ネギ), dipping sauce (つけ汁), *yuzu* citrus (ユズ), *daikon* radish and chili pepper (もみじおろし), potato starch (片栗粉)

 調理法
coagulate (凝固させる), chill (冷たい), top with (～をのせる), grate (すりおろす), boil (茹でる), dredge (まぶす), deep-fry (揚げる)

108

1 *Tofu* is a coagulated block of soymilk. The soft type is called *kinugoshi*, and the firm one is called *momen*. Both are high in protein and calcium, and low in calories.

訳 豆腐は豆乳を四角に凝固させたものです。柔らかいものを絹ごし、しっかりしたものを木綿といいます。どちらもたんぱく質とカルシウムが豊富で低カロリーです。

□ coagulate
　動 凝固させる
□ soymilk　名 豆乳
□ firm　形 かたい
□ calcium
　名 カルシウム

2 Among many *tofu* dishes is *hiyayakko*. It is chilled *tofu* topped with grated ginger, bonito flakes, Japanese green onions and soy sauce.

訳 多く存在する豆腐料理の一つが冷奴。冷やした豆腐におろし生姜、鰹節、ねぎをのせ醤油をかけたものです。

□ grate　動 すりおろす
□ bonito flakes　鰹節

Yu dofu is boiled *tofu* cubes served with a soy-based dipping sauce and garnishes such as *yuzu* citrus and *momiji oroshi* (grated *daikon* radish and chili pepper).

訳 湯豆腐は茹でた角切り豆腐で、醤油ベースのつけ汁とゆずやもみじおろし（大根と唐辛子をおろしたもの）などとともに供されます。

□ garnish　動 添える

Agedashi dofu is *tofu* that is dredged with potato starch and then deep-fried.

訳 揚げ出し豆腐は片栗粉をまぶしてたっぷりの油で揚げた豆腐です。

□ dredged with
　〜をまぶす
□ potato starch
　片栗粉

3 Popular foods made from *tofu* include *abura age*, which is a deep-fried thin sheet of *tofu*. It is used in *sushi*, noodles, *miso* soup and many other dishes.

訳 豆腐で作った人気の食材には、揚げた薄い豆腐、油揚げがあります。鮨、麺類、味噌汁ほか、多彩な料理に使われます。

副菜
Side dishes

肉じゃが **130**kcal / 里芋 **65**kcal

メニュー
37

肉じゃが と その他の煮物
Nikujaga and Other Simmered Dishes

photo：deco / PIXTA（ピクスタ）

料理のキーワード

 beef（牛肉）, potato（じゃがいも）, carrot（人参）, onion（たまねぎ）, root vegetable（根菜）, taro（里芋）, *kabocha* squash（カボチャ）, noodle-shaped *konnyaku* root cake（糸こんにゃく）

 thinly slice（薄切りにする）, simmer（煮る）

 sweet（甘い）, sticky（粘り気のある）

1 Simmered dishes in Japan are normally cooked with soy sauce, sugar, *mirin* and *sake*. The combination enhances natural flavors of ingredients. *Nikujaga* is a popular home-cooked dish made with thinly sliced beef, potatoes, carrots and onions. Noodle-shaped *konnyaku* root cake called *ito konnyaku* is often added.

□combination
名 組みあわせ
□enhance 動 高める
□shaped
〜の形状の
□process into
〜に加工する

訳 日本で煮物は通常、醤油、砂糖、みりんと酒と一緒に調理します。この組み合わせが素材の自然な風味を引き立てます。肉じゃがは牛肉の薄切り、じゃがいも、にんじん、玉ねぎで作る人気の家庭料理。糸こんにゃくと呼ばれる麺状のこんにゃくもよく加えます。

The Japanese Imperial Navy invented nikujaga based on British-style beef stew in the 19th century.

□imperial 形 帝国の
□navy 名 海軍
□invent 動 発明する

訳 肉じゃがは、日本帝国海軍が19世紀に英国風ビーフシチューをもとに生み出したものです。

2 *Satoimo* is a type of taro and is a popular root vegetable in Japan. Simmerd *Satoimo* is a great dish to enjoy the unique sticky texture of *satoimo*. Simmered *kabocha* squash (Japanese pumpkin) is another classic dish. *Kabocha* is sweeter than regular western squash.

□taro 名 タロイモ
□squash 名 カボチャ
□regular
形 規則的な

訳 里芋はタロイモの一種で、日本で人気の根菜です。里芋の煮っころがしは、その独特の粘りを楽しむのにいい料理です。カボチャ（日本のパンプキン）の煮物も伝統的な料理です。カボチャは一般の西洋瓜より甘い味がします。

副菜
Side dishes

昆布 140kcal / 牛肉 370kcal

メニュー
38

ご飯と味わう煮物
Simmered Dish for Rice

photo：hungryworks / PIXTA（ピクスタ）

料理のキーワード

 食材

shiitake mushroom（しいたけ）, fish（魚）, baby sardine（じゃこ）, shellfish（貝）, clam（蛤）, beef（牛肉）, carrot（人参）, *hijiki* seaweed（ひじき）

 調理法

simmer（煮る）

 味わい

umami（旨みのある）

説明してみよう！

52

1 There are many small simmered dishes that are served to enhance the taste of plain white rice. They are normally cooked with plenty of soy sauce, *mirin*, salt and sugar. As a result, they are highly preservative and often found in *bento* boxes.

訳 白いご飯の味わいを引き立てるための煮物の小鉢がたくさんあります。それらは通常たっぷりの醤油、みりん、塩、砂糖とともに調理します。そのため保存期間が長く、お弁当にもよく使われます。

□ enhance 動 高める
□ plain 形 平易な
□ plenty 名 多量
□ preservative 形 保存性のある

2 *Tsukudani* is made with a variety of ingredients, such as *kombu*, mushrooms, fish like baby sardine (*jako*), shellfish like clams and beef. *Tsukudani* is also a popular gift item that represents regional food culture.

訳 佃煮は昆布、きのこ、じゃこなどの魚、はまぐりなどの貝、牛肉など、多彩な食材で作られます。佃煮は地方の食文化を代表する贈答品としても人気があります。

□ sardine 名 イワシ
□ shellfish 名 貝
□ gift item 贈答品

3 *Hijiki* is a type of seaweed. It is rich in calcium and fiber, and has a pleasant texture like velvet. It is often cooked with carrots. The sweetness of carrots and the *umami* in *hijiki* enhances each other.

訳 ひじきは海草の一種です。カルシウムと繊維が豊富で、ビロードのような心地よい食感を持っています。ひじきはよくにんじんと一緒に調理します。にんじんの甘さとひじきのうま味が違いを引き立て合います。

□ seaweed 名 海藻
□ calcium 名 カルシウム
□ fiber 名 食物繊維
□ pleasant 形 心地よい
□ velvet 名 ビロード

113

副菜
Side dishes

わかめとたこ **60**kcal／なます **40**kcal

メニュー
39

酢の物
Sunomono / Vinegared dish

photo：Rhetorica / PIXTA (ピクスタ)

料理のキーワード

 食材
rice vinegar（米酢）, *wakame* seaweed（わかめ）, cucumber（きゅうり）, turnip（カブ）, crab（カニ）, octopus（タコ）, *daikon* radish（大根）, carrot（人参）, okura（オクラ）

 調理法
julienne（千切りする）, vinegar（酢で味付ける）, dress with（～であえる）

 味わい
refreshing（すがすがしい）, slippery（ぬめぬめした）, chewy（噛み応えのある）

114

説明してみよう！

1 *Sunomono* means a vinegared dish. The refreshing taste of vinegar complements other dishes. *Sunomono* may be also called *namasu*.

> **訳** 酢の物とは酢で味付けした料理のことです。さっぱりとした酢の味が他の料理を補います。酢の物はなますと呼ばれることもあります。

- □ **Vinegared**
  - 形 酢漬けの
- □ **refreshing**
  - 形 さっぱりした
- □ **complement**
  - 動 〜を補う

2 Popular ingredients include *wakame* seaweed, cucumber, turnip, crab and octopus. *Kouhaku* (red *and white*) *namasu* is made with julienned *daikon* radish and carrots. Because of the festive colors of red and white, it is eaten during the New Year celebration.

> **訳** 人気の素材には、わかめ、きゅうり、かぶ、かに、たこなどがあります。紅白なますは千切りした大根と人参で作ります。その赤白のおめでたい色合いから、新年に食べられます。

- □ **turnip** 名 カブ
- □ **julienned**
  - 千切りした
- □ **festive** 形 お祝いの

3 Seaweed is a common ingredient for *sunomono*. *Mozuku* and *mekabu* both have a okra-like slippery texture, which is said to be healthy. Chewy *mekabu* comes from the same plant as leafy *wakame*, and it is near the root.

> **訳** 海草は酢の物によく使われる素材です。もずくとめかぶはどちらもオクラのようなぬめりを持っており、それが健康にいいといわれています。かみごたえのあるめかぶはワカメと同じ植物から取れますが、これは根に近い部分です。

- □ **okra** 名 オクラ
- □ **slippery**
  - 形 すべりやすい、ぬめりのある
- □ **leafy** 形 葉っぱ状の

副菜
Side dishes

菜の花のからし和え **75**kcal / ほうれん草の胡麻和え **75**kcal

和え物
Aemono / Dish with Dressings

photo：Caito / PIXTA（ピクスタ）

料理のキーワード

 食材
rape blossom（菜の花）, spinach（ほうれん草）, Japanese *karashi* mustard（からし）, sesame seed（すりごま）, *tofu*（豆腐）, red pickled plum（梅干し）, vinegar（酢）

 調理法
mash（すりつぶす）, toast（焼く）, grind（細かく砕く）, blanch（湯がく）, dress with（〜で和える）

 味わい
nuttiness（ナッツ風味の）, richness（濃厚な）, spicy（辛い）

説明してみよう！

54

1 *Aemono* means dishes with dressings.
Like *sunomono*, they are small but
add another flavor dimension to the
table. There are different ingredients
of *aemono* dressings.

訳 和え物とはドレッシングを混ぜ合わせた料理です。酢の物同
様、小さいながらも食卓に新たな風味の側面を与えます。和
え物のドレッシングには様々な素材があります。

Shira ae is made with mashed *tofu*,
goma ae with toasted and ground
sesame seeds, *ume ae* with pickled
plum, *miso ae* with miso, and *sumiso
ae* with *miso* and vinegar (*su*). *Dashi*
is often added to the dressing too.

訳 白和えはすりつぶした豆腐、胡麻和えは炒ってすりおろした
ゴマ、梅和えは梅干し、味噌和えは味噌、酢味噌和えは味噌
と酢で作ります。ドレッシングにはよく、出汁も加えます。

2 One of the most popular *aemono*
dishes is *nanohana no karashi ae*.
Highly seasonal rape blossoms are
dressed with spicy Japanese mustard
karashi and soy sauce. *Horenso no
goma ae* is another classic dish.
Blanched spinach is dressed with
sesame seeds, soy sauce and sugar.
The nuttiness and richness of the
sesame complement the taste of spinach.

訳 最も人気の和え物料理の一つに菜の花のからし和えがありま
す。季節性の高い菜の花を、日本のマスタードであるからし
と醤油で和えたものです。ほうれん草の胡麻和えも代表的な
料理です。湯がいたほうれん草をゴマ、醤油と砂糖で和えた
ものです。ゴマのナッツのような風味と濃厚さがほうれん草
の味を引き立てます。

□dressing
　名 ドレッシング
□dimension
　名 側面

□mash　動 すりつぶす
□ground sesame
　すりごま
□pickled plum
　梅干し

□rape blossoms
　菜の花
□blanch　動 湯がく
□spinach
　名 ホウレンソウ
□nuttiness
　名 ナッツの風味
□richness　名 濃厚さ

117

副菜
Side dishes

こんにゃく **10**kcal /豆腐 **65**kcal

メニュー
41

田楽
Dengaku / Miso-glazed Grill

料理のキーワード

 食材
konnyaku root cake (こんにゃく), *daikon* radish (大根), eggplant (ナス), *yuzu* citrus peel (ユズの皮), buds of *sansho* pepper (山椒の芽)

 調理法
skewer (串にさす), grill (焼く), glaze (塗る), flavor with (味付けする)

55

1 *Dengaku* or *miso dengaku* is a dish of skewered ingredients that are grilled and glazed with *miso*. The most classic ingredients of *dengaku* are *tofu*, *konnyaku* root cake, *daikon radish* and eggplant.

☐skewer
　動 串に刺す
☐glaze　動 塗る
☐eggplant　名 ナス

訳 田楽または味噌田楽は、串にした素材を焼いて味噌を塗ったものです。最も代表的な田楽の素材は豆腐、こんにゃく、大根、ナスです。

The *miso* glaze is flavored with sugar and *mirin*. *Yuzu* citrus peel or *kinome* (buds of *sansho* pepper) is often added to the glaze. There is a wide variety of regional *dengaku* that reflect the local food culture.

☐bud　名 芽

訳 塗る味噌は砂糖とみりんで味をつけます。柚子の皮や木の芽（山椒の芽）もよく味噌に加えます。田楽には地方の食文化を反映した多彩な種類があります。

2 *Dengaku* was named around the 13th century after the unique looking dancers in white outfits on single stilts. They were called *dengaku hoshi* and performed in the rice field for a great harvest. The shape of skewered tofu *dengaku* resembled them.

☐outfit　名 服装
☐single stilts
　高足（一本の棒に乗って飛び跳ねる芸）
☐resemble
　動 〜に似ている

訳 田楽の名は、13世紀辺りに白い衣装を着け一本の高足で踊る踊り手の姿から来ています。彼らは田楽法師と呼ばれ、豊作を祈り田んぼで踊りました。串に刺さった豆腐田楽の形が彼らに似ていたのです。

のり
Nori Seaweed

海外で海苔（乾燥した海草）は、巻き鮨でしか見ないかもしれません。
しかし日本では、海苔は鮨、おにぎり、餅、せんべいを包むものとして使われますね。そば、ラーメンその他多くの料理にも、トッピングや飾りとしてよく用いられます。

海苔にはそのまま、焼いたもの、味付けされたもの、粉末状にしたものなど、色々な形があります。ふりかけは刻んだ海苔を卵や鰹節など他の乾燥素材と合わせたものです。通常白いご飯の味付けに使われます。海苔は加工して佃煮にもなります。

海苔はとても健康的な食べ物でもあります。カロリーが非常に低く、繊維、鉄分、カルシウム、ビタミン A、B、C に富んでいます。

You may see *nori* (dried seaweed) only in *sushi* rolls outside Japan. But in japan, it is used as a wrapper in *sushi*, *onigiri*, *mochi* and rice crackers. It is also often found as a topping or a garnish in *soba* noodles, *ramen* and many other dishes.

There are various forms of *nori*, such as plain, toasted, flavored and powdered. *Furikake* is chopped *nori* mixed with other dry ingredients such as egg and, bonito flakes. It is primarily used to season plain rice. *Nori* is also processed to make *tsukudani*.

Nori is a very healthy food too. It is very low in calories and rich in fiber, iron, calcium, vitamin A, B and C.

漬物

Tsukemono

その健康性の高さから、ピクルスは世界的に人気が高まっています。日本は多彩な健康的なピクルスを誇り、漬物（香の物、お新香）と呼んでいます。

日本の漬物は、他国では見られない独自の製法でつくられます。ぬか漬けは米ぬかと塩で作った漬物のこと。ぬかはビタミンB1、乳酸菌とその他の栄養素が豊富なため健康的です。たくあんは大根のぬか漬けのことです。その鮮明な黄色はその成分からくる自然なものです。粕漬けは日本酒か、みりんの澱（日本酒やみりんの副産物）、塩と砂糖で作ります。澱が食材に旨みを与えてくれます。粕漬けは、さばや鮭などの魚を焼く前に漬けるのにも使われます。

Pickles are becoming popular globally for their health benefits. Japan boasts a diverse range of healthy pickles called *tsukemono* (*kou no mono, oshinko*.)

There are unique ways to make pickles that you don't find outside Japan. *Nukazuke* is pickles made with rice bran (*nuka*) and salt. It is healthy because *nuka* is rich in vitamin B1, lactic acid and other nutrients. *Takuan* is a *nukazuke daikon*. The bright yellow color comes naturally from its own chemicals. *Kasuzuke* is made with *sake* or *mirin* lees (a byproduct of *sake* or *mirin* production), salt and sugar. The lees add *umami* to the ingredients. *Kasuzuke* is also used to pickle fish such as mackerel and salmon before they are grilled.

日本のスープ
Japanese Soups

「一汁三菜」の最後の一品は汁物です。日常的に食卓に並ぶ味噌汁や、フォーマルな場にも出される吸い物など、和食の汁物について紹介してみましょう。

汁物―Facts

photo：マーボー / PIXTA（ピクスタ）

- 味噌の年間平均消費量（annual average miso consumption in Japan）—
  5.2kg/世帯（householding）
- 味噌汁の起源（the origin of miso soup）—
  鎌倉時代（Kamakura period, 12th century）

参照：総務省「家計調査 2016~2018 年平均」

---

① Soup is called *shirumono*
汁物といわれるスープ

56

Soup is called *shirumono* in *washoku*. It is an essential part of the Japanese diet. The most popular type of *shirumono* is *miso* soup. It is a part of *ichiju sansai*, and served at home on a daily basis.

□diet 名 食生活
□on a daily basis 名 日常的に

 和食ではスープのことを汁物といいます。日本人の食生活に不可欠なものです。もっとも一般的なタイプの汁物は味噌汁です。これは一汁三菜の一要素で、家庭で日常的に出されます。

In our modern life, people do not have time to make *miso* soup. If you go to a supermarket, you can find a wide range of instant *miso* soup.

□range 名 範囲

 現代の生活では味噌汁を作る時間がなかなかありません。スーパーでは様々な種類のインスタント味噌汁が並んでいます。

② Variations of *shirumono*
汁物の種類

Another popular *shirumono* is *suimono*. It is typically served at a formal dinner to enjoy with *sake*, whereas *miso* soup is to enjoy with rice. *Ushiojiru* is a soup made by simmering seafood such as sea bream and clams. It is lightly flavored with salt. They say fishermen invented the recipe.

□ formal
形 フォーマルな
□ whereas
接 ～に対して
□ sea bream　鯛
□ clam　名 ハマグリ
□ fishermen　名 漁師
□ invent
動 考案する

 吸い物も人気の汁物です。味噌汁がご飯と味わうものなのに対し、吸い物はフォーマルな食事で酒の肴として楽しまれます。潮汁は鯛やハマグリなどの魚介類を煮て作った汁です。軽く塩で味をつけます。漁師が生み出したレシピと言われています。

③ Beautiful bowls
美しい碗

Japanese soup bowls have a long tradition of simplicity, beauty and attention to detail. They are called *wan*. It is typically a lacquer ware made of wood that comes with or without a lid. Its hue would be red, brown or black, which enhances the colors of ingredients inside.

□ simplicity
名 簡素さ
□ attention to
～への注意
□ lacquer ware
漆器
□ lid　名 蓋
□ hue　名 色合い

 日本のスープボウルは簡素さと美しさは長きに渡る伝統で、細部にまで気が配られています。これらは椀（わん）と呼ばれます。椀は通常蓋つきか蓋なしの木製の漆器です。その色合いは、中の食材の色を引き立てる赤、茶、黒が一般的です。

漆器（lacquer ware）とは、漆といわれる漆の木の樹液で塗られた器（wares coated with sap of Japanese lacquer）のことです！

🍲 豆腐とわかめ **30**kcal

メニュー
44

味噌汁
Misoshiru / Miso Soup

マーボー / PIXTA（ピクスタ）

料理のキーワード

 食材
wakame seaweed（わかめ）**, clam**（あさり）**, root vegetable**（根菜）**, mushrooms**（きのこ）**, deep-fried tofu**（油揚げ）

 調理法
simmer（煮る）

 調理器具・器
soup bowl（汁椀）

 味わい
sweet（甘い）**, nutty**（ナッツ風味の）

124

説明してみよう！

57

1 *Miso* soup is made of *dashi* stock and *miso*. It is an excellent source of protein. *Miso* is fermented soybeans with or without other types of grain. The process of fermentation makes protein in soybeans more absorbable.

訳 味噌汁は出汁と味噌で作ります。味噌汁は優れたタンパク源です。味噌は大豆をそのままあるいは他の穀物と一緒に発酵させたものです。発酵を通じて大豆のたんぱく質がより吸収されやすくなります。

You can add a wide variety of ingredients to make *miso* soup, such as *tofu*, *aburaage* (deep-fried thin sheets of *tofu*), *wakame* seaweed, clams, root vegetables, mushrooms, fish and shellfish.

訳 味噌汁は、豆腐、油揚げ、わかめ、あさり、根菜、きのこ、魚介類など、様々な食材と一緒に作ることができます。

2 Each recipe of *miso* soup reflects the regional food culture and the family tradition.

訳 一つひとつの味噌汁のレシピが地方の食文化と家庭の伝統を反映します。

Sweet white *miso* made with soybeans and rice is classic in Kyoto. The area around Nagoya prefers saltier red miso made only with soybeans. In Kyusyu, nutty *mugi miso* (barley miso) made with barley is popular.

訳 京都では、大豆と米で作る甘い白味噌が定番です。名古屋近郊では大豆だけで作る塩気の強い赤味噌が好まれます。九州ではナッツ風味の麦味噌が人気です。

□source 名 源
□fermented
　形 発酵した
□grain 名 穀物
□fermentation
　名 発酵
□absorbable
　形 吸収性のある

□root vegetable
　根菜

□reflect 動 反映する

□saltier salty
　比 塩辛い
□nutty
　形 ナッツ風味の
□barley 名 麦

125

15kcal

メニュー
45

吸い物
Suimono / Clear Soup

photo：マーボー / PIXTA（ピクスタ）

料理のキーワード

 食材

fish（魚）, shellfish（貝）, meatball（肉団子）, *tofu* skin（豆腐）, chicken（鶏肉）, seaweed（海藻）, *siitake* mushroom（しいたけ）, *yuzu* citrus peel（ユズの皮）, *sansho* pepper leaf（木の芽）, Japanese ginger（ミョウガ）

 味わい

clear（澄んだ）

126

58

1 *Suimono* is another popular soup in Japan. The biggest difference from *miso* soup is that *suimono* is a clear soup without *miso*. The liquid is made of *dashi*, salt and soy sauce.

□clear 形 透明な
□liquid 名 汁

訳 吸い物も日本で人気の汁物です。味噌汁との一番大きな違いは、味噌を使わない透明な汁であることです。汁は出汁、塩と醤油で作ります。

There are three solid ingredients. *Wandane* is protein-based, such as fish, shellfish, *shinjo* (fish or shellfish meatballs), *tofu*, *yuba* (*tofu* skin) and chicken. *Tsuma* is something that complements *wandane* like vegetable, seaweed and mushroom. *Suikuchi* adds fragrance to the bowl. *Yuzu* citrus peel, *kinome* (*sansho* pepper leaves) and *myoga* (Japanese ginger) are often used.

□solid ingredients 具材
□tofu skin ゆば
□complement 動 補う
□fragrance 名 香り
□peel 名 皮

訳 具材には3つあります。椀種は魚、貝類、しんじょ、豆腐、ゆば、鶏などのたんぱく質系です。つまとは野菜、海藻、きのこなどの椀種を補うものです。吸い口は椀に香りを加えます。柚子の皮、木の芽、ミョウガなどがよく使われます。

Suimono is typically served as a part of a formal *kaiseki* menu.

訳 典型的に吸い物は会席料理の一部として出されます。

2 *Osumashi* or *sumashijiru* is similar to *suimono*, but it simply means a clear soup without any rules about the ingredients.

□be similar to ～に似ている

訳 お澄まし、もしくは澄まし汁は吸い物と似ていますが、単に透明な汁という意味で、具材についての決まりはありません。

127

鍋料理 Hot Pot

鍋物は単なる食事以上の意味をもつ料理です。「鍋奉行」や「まち娘」などの説明と一緒に、鍋を囲んだ家族、友人との交流の風景を紹介してみましょう。

photo：taa / PIXTA（ピクスタ）

鍋―Facts

- 日本人がよく食べる鍋（3 most cooked hot pot by Japanese）―
  ①おでん（*oden*）　②すき焼き（*sukiyaki*）　③キムチ鍋（kimchi hot pot）
- 日本人が好きなおでん種（the most favorite oden topping of Japanese）―
  大根（*daikon* radish）

参照：「紀文鍋白書 2019」

① Hot pot is a communal process
鍋物は共同で生み出すもの

⬇59

Hot pot (*nabe*) is a communal dish that is usually shared with family and friends. A gas or electric burner is placed on the table and you are ready to cook a delicious meal together over a boiling broth.

 鍋物は家族や友人とシェアする共同性の高い料理です。ガスや電気バーナーを卓上に置けば、美味しい食事をぐらぐら煮立つ出汁で一緒に調理する準備は万端です。

You prepare tableside and eat as soon as the ingredients are cooked, and keep adding more ingredients. After all the ingredients are gone, rice or noodles are added to enjoy the leftover broth.

 具材が調理でき次第食べ、さらに具材を追加します。全ての具材を食べ終わったら、米や麺を加えて残りの出汁を味わいます。

□ communal
　形 共同の
□ electric burner
　電気バーナー
□ broth　名 だし

□ tableside
　副 テーブルのわきに
□ leftover　形 残りの

128

② Cooking *nabe* reveals who you are
人柄を表す鍋料理

People joke about the personality of each person involved in making nabe. Different personalities are named after titles of people in feudal Japan.
For example, *nabe bugyo* is a type of person who wants to control everything from the order of ingredients to put into the pot, when to eat, and so on (*Bugyo means* governor).

 鍋料理を囲む各人の性格について皆ジョークを飛ばします。それぞれの性格は、日本の封建時代の肩書きにならっています。例えば鍋奉行は、具材を入れる順番から食べるタイミングまで、全てコントロールしたいタイプ（奉行とは統治者のこと）。

□ joke 動 冗談を言う
□ be named after
　〜にちなんで名づけられる
□ title 名 肩書き
□ feudal
　形 封建時代の
□ governor
　名 統治者

③ *Donabe*
土鍋

Donabe is the classic earthenware for nabe cooking. The clay pot can be placed directly over a flame and it keeps a high temperature well.

 土鍋は鍋に使われる伝統的な土製の調理器具です。土鍋は炎の上に直接置くことができ、高温をしっかり維持します。

□ earthenware
　名 陶器
□ clay pot 土器
□ flame 名 炎
□ temperature
　名 温度

出来上がりを待つだけの女の子（a girl who does not do anything but wait for food to be served）を「まち娘（a town/waiting girl）」とも呼びます！

鍋料理
Hot Pot

メニュー
46

寄せ鍋
Yosenabe / Hot Pot with Various Ingredients

photo：ささざわ / PIXTA（ピクスタ）

料理のキーワード

seafood（魚介類）, chicken（鶏肉）, pork（豚肉）, vegetable（野菜）, Chinese cabbage（白菜）, Japanese green onion（ネギ）, chrysanthemums leaf（春菊）, mushroom（きのこ）, *shirataki* noodles（しらたき）, cooking liquid（煮汁）, chicken bones（鳥の骨）, dipping sauce of vinegar, soy sauce, and citrus juice（ポン酢のタレ）

cook（煮込む）, flavor with（〜で味をつける）

調理器具・器 hot pot（鍋）

説明してみよう！

60

1 *Yose* means to gather up and *nabe* means hot pot. *Yosenabe* is a hot pot that can be made with any kinds of ingredients. The cooking liquid is made with *dashi*. It may be flavored with soy sauce, salt or *miso*.

訳 「寄せ」は集める、「鍋」はホットポットを意味します。寄せ鍋はどんな材料を使ってもできる鍋料理です。煮汁はだしベース。醤油、塩か味噌などで味付けします。

□ gather up
　〜を集める
□ cooking liquid
　煮汁

2 Popular ingredients include *tofu*, seafood, chicken and pork. Vegetables like Chinese cabbage and chrysanthemum leaves are often used. Mushrooms and *shirataki* (noodle-shaped jelly-like food *konnyaku* root cake) are also essential.

訳 よく使われる具材は豆腐、魚介類、鶏肉、豚肉です。白菜、春菊などの野菜は頻繁に使われます。きのこやしらたき（ゼリー状のたべもの、こんにゃくの麺状のもの）も欠かせない素材です。

□ Chinese cabbage
　白菜

3 *Mizutaki* is similar to *yosenabe*, but the cooking liquid is flavored with the ingredient itself. Typically it is made with chicken bones, its meat and vegetables. *Ponzu* is served together as a dipping sauce.

訳 水炊きは寄せ鍋に似ていますが、煮汁は具材自体で味をつけます。代表的な水炊きは鶏の骨と肉と野菜で作ります。つけ汁としてポン酢を一緒に出します。

鍋料理
Hot Pot

90kcal　¥～300

メニュー
47

おでん
Oden / Hot Pot with Dengaku Ingredients

photo：ささざわ / PIXTA（ピクスタ）

料理のキーワード

食材

cooking liquid（煮汁）, *konnyaku* root cake（こんにゃく）, ground fish and yam cake（はんぺん）, *shrataki* noodles（しらたき）minced fish cake（つみれ）, fried fish cake（さつま揚げ）, boiled egg（ゆで卵）, *daikon* radish（大根）

調理法

cook（煮込む）

調理器具・器

hot pot（鍋）

132

説明してみよう!

61

1 *Oden* is a very popular classic hot pot. It is a derivative of *dengaku* (skewered food glazed with *miso*). The same ingredients as *dengaku* were cooked in a pot with *miso*, and people began to call it *oden*.

訳▶おでんはとても人気のある代表的な鍋ものです。田楽（味噌を塗った串料理）から派生したものです。田楽と同じ素材を鍋で味噌と一緒に煮込み、おでんと呼ぶようになりました。

□ derivative
形 派生した

2 A soy-based cooking liquid is very popular now, and it is called *kantoni* (Kanto-style simmered dish) in the Kansai region.

訳▶今では醤油ベースの煮汁が一般的になり、関西ではそれは関東煮と呼ばれます。

□ cooking liquid
煮汁

3 You can find *oden* at specialized restaurants, nostalgic street stalls and convenience stores. *Oden* is highly regional and home cooks have their own recipes.

訳▶おでんは専門店、懐かしの路上の屋台、コンビニで見つかります。おでんは地域性が高く、各家庭でそれぞれのレシピを持っています。

105kcal ¥～5,000

メニュー 48

すきやき
Sukiyaki / Beef Hot Pot

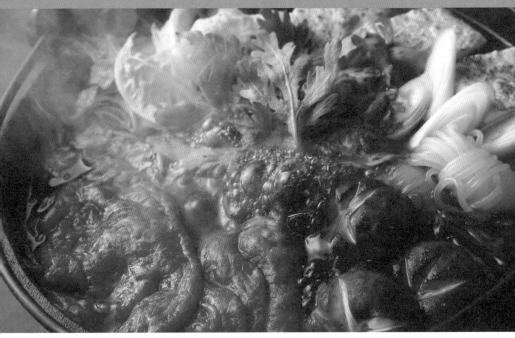

photo：taa / PIXTA (ピクスタ)

料理のキーワード

 食材
beef (牛肉), Chinese cabbage (白菜), chrysanthemums greens (春菊), Japanese green onion (ネギ), *shiitake* mushroom (しいたけ), baked *tofu* (焼き豆腐), *shirataki* noodles (しらたき), raw beaten egg (溶き卵)

 調理法
thinly slice (薄切り), cook (煮る), dip into (浸ける)

 調理器具・器
shallow iron pot (浅い鉄鍋), bowl (椀)

説明してみよう！

62

1 *Sukiyaki* is thinly sliced beef and other ingredients cooked in a shallow iron pot. The Japanese began eating beef only after 1860s when the western culture flooded into the country. *Sukiyaki* is now a very popular dish.

🈂 すき焼きは薄切りの牛肉と他の食材を浅い鉄鍋で煮たものです。日本人は1860年代に西洋文化が急速に流入するまで牛肉を食べませんでした。すき焼きは今ではとても人気の料理です。

□ thinly sliced
薄切りの

□ shallow 名 浅い

□ iron pot 鉄鍋

□ flood into
～になだれ込む

2 Classic ingredients are beef, Chinese cabbage, chrysanthemum leaves, Japanese green onion, *shiitake*, baked *tofu* and *shirataki*. In the Kanto region, they make *warishita*, which is a mixture of soy sauce, sugar, *sake* and *mirin*, and add it to the pot. In the Kansai region, these seasonings are directly added to the pot.

🈂 典型的な素材は牛肉、白菜、春菊、ねぎ、しいたけ、焼き豆腐、しらたきです。関東では、醤油、砂糖、酒、みりんを合わせた割り下を作り、鍋に入れます。関西では、これらの調味料は直接鍋に入れます。

□ seasoning
名 調味料

3 Once cooked, the ingredients are dipped into a bowl of a raw beaten egg. The hot food cooks the egg and the egg enriches the flavor of the dish.

🈂 調理された具材は、溶き卵に浸けます。熱い具材が卵に火を入れ、卵は味に深みを与えてくれます。

□ beaten egg
溶き卵

□ enrich
動 濃厚にする

鍋料理
Hot Pot

メニュー 49 しゃぶしゃぶ
Shabu Shabu / Pork Hot Pot

photo：freeangle / PIXTA（ピクスタ）

料理のキーワード

 食材

pork（豚肉）, beef（牛肉）, lamb（子羊）, fish（魚）,boiling water（煮立った湯）, Chinese cabbage（白菜）, Japanese green onion（ネギ）, *shiitake* mushroom（しいたけ）, carrot（人参）, dipping sauce of vinegar, soy sauce, and citrus juice（ポン酢のタレ）,creamy white sesame sauce（ごまだれ）

 調理法

boil（茹でる）, swish（振る）, dip into（浸ける）

 調理器具・器

hot pot（鍋）

1 *Shabu shabu* is a fun hot pot to share with family or friends. A paper-thin slice of beef or pork is dropped into boiling water in the pot on the table, and retrieved it before it loses flavor to the liquid.

□ **paper-thin**
　紙の薄さの
□ **retrieve**
　動 取り出す

訳 しゃぶしゃぶは家族や友人と分け合う楽しい鍋料理です。紙のように薄く切った牛肉や豚肉を、卓上で煮立ったお湯に入れ、風味が液体に溶け出す前に引き上げます。

The sound you make when you swish meat in hot water sounds like *shabu shabu*. It is made with other regional ingredients such as fish and lamb.

□ **swish** 動 振る
□ **lamb**
　名 子羊（の肉）

訳 肉をお湯の中で振る際に立つ音がしゃぶしゃぶと聞こえます。地方により魚や子羊などでも作ります。

2 Vegetables are added to the pot to balance with the rich flavor of the meat. Chinese cabbage, Japanese green onion, *shiitake*, carrots and *tofu* are typical items. The cooked ingredients are eaten with a dipping sauce. It is usually made with *ponzu* (a sauce made with soy sauce, vinegar and citrus juice) or creamy white sesame.

□ **balance with**
　〜とバランスを取る

訳 濃厚な肉の旨味とバランスをとる野菜も鍋に加えます。白菜、ネギ、しいたけ、人参、豆腐などがよく使わる食材です。調理された具材はつけ汁で食べます。通常つけ汁はポン酢（醤油、酢と柑橘類の果汁で作ったソース）かクリーミーな白ごまで作ります。

鍋料理
Hot Pot

🍽 35kcal 👛 ¥〜1,000

湯豆腐
Yudofu / Tofu Hot Pot

photo：ささざわ / PIXTA（ピクスタ）

料理のキーワード

 食材
boiling broth（煮立った出汁）, *tofu*（豆腐）, chopped scallions（刻みねぎ）, bonito flakes（鰹節）, grated *daikon* radish（大根おろし）, grated ginger（おろし生姜）, citrus juice（かんきつ果汁）

 調理法
flavor with（〜で味をつける）

 調理器具・器
hot pot（鍋）

 味わい
simple（シンプル）, fluffy（ふわふわ）, silky（すべすべ）, dense（密度の高い）, hot（温かい）, aromatic（香り高い）

1 *Yudofu* is a very simple hot pot, but it is a great way to enjoy the deliciousness of *tofu*. Also, it is an important vegetarian dish eaten by Zen monks. *Tofu* is cooked in a boiling broth flavored with *kombu*. Apart from regular hot pot dishes, there are no other ingredients added to the pot.

□deliciousness
名 おいしさ
□Zen monk 名 禅僧
□broth 名 出汁
□apart from
〜は別として

訳 湯豆腐はとてもシンプルな鍋ものですが、豆腐の美味しさを味わうのにとてもいい料理です。また禅僧にとって大事なベジタリアン料理です。豆腐は昆布で味付けしたお湯で調理します。通常の鍋物とは違い、それ以外の食材は加えません。

2 There are mainly two types of *tofu*. *Kinugoshi* has a fluffy, silky texture. *Momen* is denser and firmer. You can choose either one of them to make *yudofu*.

□fluffy
形 ふわふわした
□silky
形 すべすべした
□dense
形 密度の高い

訳 豆腐は水分の含有量により主に2種類あります。絹ごしはふわふわ、すべすべとした食感です。木綿はより密度が高くしっかりしています。湯豆腐にはどちらも使えます。

3 The hot *tofu* is typically eaten with a soy sauce-based dipping sauce. It is usually flavored with aromatic garnishes, such as chopped Japanese green onion, bonito flakes, grated *daikon radish* or ginger, *shiso*, *wasabi* and citrus juice.

□chopped 刻んだ
□grate 動 すりおろす

訳 熱々の豆腐は通常醤油ベースのつけ汁で食べます。つけ汁には刻みネギ、鰹節、大根おろし、おろし生姜、しそ、わさび、かんきつ果汁などの香り豊かな薬味で風味を加えます。

居酒屋文化
The *Izakaya* Culture

居酒屋は海外のタバーンやガストロパブに似たカジュアルな飲食店。色々な日本料理を味わいながら、居酒屋ならではのユニークなサービスを体験できます。

例えば席に着くと手を拭く為のおしぼりが出てきます（夏は冷たく冬は暖かいもの）。食事を通じて食べ物と飲み物をオーダーできます。金額と時間限定の飲み放題は、割安価格を求める観光客にはうれしい選択肢です。外国人訪問者の中には、チップ制度のない日本の慣習とはいえ、頼んでいないお通しがチャージされる事に驚く人もいるかもしれません。

Izakaya is a casual eatery similar to a tavern or gastropub. You can taste a variety of Japanese foods and experience the features that are unique to an *izakaya*.

For instance, *oshibori* (a wet towel offered for cleaning hands) is served right after you settle down (cold one in summer, warm one in winter). You can keep ordering food and drink throughout the meal. *Nominodai* (all you can drink) has a set price with a time limit. It is a welcoming option for value-seeking tourists. Foreign visitors may be surprised to be charged for *otooshi* (small appetizers served before ordering food), even though it is customary that these are included in the bill as a service charge, because there is no tipping system in Japan.

3章

飲みもの

Beverages

日本茶
Japanese Tea

中国茶や紅茶とも違った製法で作られ、飲み方のスタイルも異なる日本茶の味わいや効能、製法によって区別される日本茶の種類について紹介しましょう。

photo：まちゃー / PIXTA（ピクスタ）

日本茶 ― Facts

- 生産量の多い県（3 top producing prefectures）
  ―①静岡県（Shizuoka）　②鹿児島県（Kagoshima）　③三重県（Mie）
- 1人当たりの年間消費量（annual per capita consumption）― × 170

参照：農林水産省「茶をめぐる情勢（令和元年 6 月）」、総務省「平成 30 年家計調査」

① Japanese tea is unique
日本茶は独自のもの

🔽65

Tea is an essential part of Japanese culture. Japanese tea (*nihoncha*) is unique. Tea leaves are steamed as soon as they are picked. Steaming keeps their color beautiful green.

 お茶は日本文化の重要な一部です。日本茶は独自のものです。お茶の葉は摘んですぐに蒸します。蒸すことでその美しい緑色が損なわれません。

□ essential
形 重要な
□ steam　動 蒸す
□ ferment
動 発酵する

Also, unlike Chinese or black tea, they are not fermented. As a result, Japanese tea does not lose the delicate tastes of the tea leaves such as *umami*, *nigami* (bitterness), *shibumi* (astringency) and *amami* (sweetness).

 また中国茶や紅茶と違い発酵させません。その結果、葉の本来の旨味、苦味、渋み、甘みといった繊細な味を失うことがありません。

□ ferment
動 発酵する
□ astringency
名 渋み

142

② Japanese tea is healthy
健康的である日本茶

Japanese green tea has multiple health benefits. For example, it contains less caffeine than coffee, but enough to increase mental clarity. Also, it has calming effects to counterbalance the stimulating effects of caffeine. It is rich in antioxidants called catechins too.

 訳 日本茶には多くの健康効果があります。例えばカフェインはコーヒーより少ないのに、十分な覚醒作用があります。また日本茶には、カフェインの覚醒作用の刺激とのバランスをとる、沈静効果もあります。抗酸化物質カテキンも豊富です。

- □ multiple 形 複数の
- □ benefit 名 利益
- □ caffeine 名 カフェイン
- □ mental clarity 意識覚醒
- □ calming 形 沈静する
- □ counterbalance 名 つり合い
- □ antioxidant 名 抗酸化物質

③ The main Japanese tea production regions
日本茶の名産地

There are many regions that produce high-quality Japanese tea throughout the country. The most well-known regions include Shizuoka Prefecture, Uji in Kyoto, Sayama in Saitama and Yame in Fukuoka. The Japanese small teapot is called *kyusu* and the tea cup is called *yunomi*.

訳 日本全国に良質の日本茶生産地域が存在します。最も名高い地域には、静岡県、京都の宇治、埼玉の狭山、福岡の八女などがあります。日本の小さなティーポットを急須といい、ティーカップは湯呑みと呼びます。

- □ high-quality 良質の
- □ throughout the country 全国に

おいしさを十分に味わうため（to taste tea flavors to the fullest）、砂糖やミルクは加えない（No sugar or milk is added）ことも日本茶のポイントです！

 飲み物① 日本茶
Japanese Tea

 5kcal

日本茶の種類
Types of Japanese Tea

photo：株式会社デザインメイト / PIXTA（ピクスタ）

料理のキーワード

 食材　tea leaf（茶葉）, barley（麦）

 調理法　steam（蒸す）, roast（炒る）

 調理器具・器　tea cup（湯呑）, tea pot（急須）

 味わい　full-flavored（コクがある）, aromatic（香り高い）, refreshing（すっきりとした）, *umami*（旨み）, sweetness（甘さ）, astringent（渋い）, toasty（香ばしい）, nutty（ナッツ風味）

1 The most popular type of Japanese tea is *sencha*. *Fukamushi* is made with leaves that were steamed for a longer time than *sencha*. As a result, it is less astringent and full-flavored than *sencha*.

□astringent 形 渋い
□full-flavored 形 こくがある

訳 日本茶で一番人気が高いのが煎茶です。深蒸しは煎茶より蒸し時間を長くしたものです。そのため味わいは渋みが抑えめで、よりこくがあります。

2 *Bancha* is made from harder leaves than *sencha*. The refreshing taste makes it the second most popular tea in Japan. *Gyokuro* is a premium tea. The young buds are grown under screens for a few weeks before harvest. The resulting tea is full of *umami* and sweetness.

□premium 形 高級な
□bud 名 芽
□screen 名 遮蔽物
□harvest 名 収穫

訳 番茶は煎茶より固めの葉で作ります。そのさっぱりとした味わいから二番目に人気の高いお茶です。玉露は高級茶です。収穫前の数週間、若芽を光から遮って育てます。その結果生まれるお茶は、旨味と甘みがたっぷりです。

3 *Hojicha* is a roasted tea after the leaves have been steamed. It is toasty and lower in caffeine. *Genmaicha* is *bancha* or *sencha* mixed with roasted and popped rice with a nutty aroma. *Mugicha* is roasted barley tea. Served chilled, it is a summer time favorite.

□toasty 形 香ばしい
□pop 動 はじける
□barley 名 大麦

訳 ほうじ茶は葉を蒸した後に炒ったお茶です。香ばしくカフェインが低めです。玄米茶は番茶か煎茶を、炒ってはじけた米と合わせたもので、ナッツのような香りです。麦茶は炒った大麦のお茶。冷やして出される、夏に人気のお茶です。

飲み物①

日本茶
Japanese Tea

メニュー
53

抹茶と茶道
Matcha and Tea Ceremony

photo：yazawa / PIXTA（ピクスタ）

料理のキーワード

 食材　tea leaf（茶葉）

 調理法　powder（粉末にする）, grind (ground)（すり砕く）, steam（蒸す）, whisk（茶筅）

 調理器具・器　serving vessels（茶器）, tea cup（茶碗）

 味わい　subtle bitterness（微かな苦み）, deep aroma（深い香り）, fine froth（細かい泡）, *umami*（旨みのある）

146

説明してみよう！

1 *Matcha* is powdered green tea. Young buds are grown in shade like *gyokuro*, but it is ground after being steamed.

> 訳 抹茶は粉末状の緑茶です。お茶の若芽を玉露と同じく日陰で育て、蒸した後に粉にします。

To make *matcha* tea, put the powder in a teacup and gently whisk it with a special tool called *chasen* until a fine froth appears on the surface. *Matcha*'s rich *umami* is enhanced by the subtle bitterness and deep aroma.

> 訳 抹茶を点てるには、粉を茶器に入れ、丁寧に茶筅という道具できめ細かい泡が表面にできるまで混ぜます。ほのかな苦味と深い香りが、その豊かな旨味を引き立てます。

□ powder
形 粉末にした
□ ground 動 挽く
□ whisk 動 かき回す
□ froth 名 泡
□ subtle 形 ほのかな

2 The traditional Japanese tea ceremony is called *sado* or *chado*. It is the occasion of preparing and serving tea in a sparsely yet beautifully decorated quiet room.

> 訳 日本の伝統的なお茶会を茶道といいます。簡素ながらも美しく物静かな部屋で、お茶を用意して出す席のことです。

The host aims to offer the most wonderful time for the guests through his/her smooth movement, beautiful tea bowls, delicious sweets and carefully made *matcha* green tea. Tea ceremony represents the essence of the Japanese-style hospitality *omotenashi*.

> 訳 主人は滑らかな動作や、美しい茶器、美味しい食べ物や細心の注意を払って点てたお茶を通じて、お客が最高の時間を過ごせることを目指します。茶道は日本のホスピタリティであるおもてなしの真髄を象徴します。

□ tea ceremony
茶会
□ sparsely
副 まばらに
□ decorated
形 装飾された

□ tea bowls 名 茶器
□ hospitality 名 おもてなし

147

日本のアルコール
Alcohol Beverages of Japan

日本人にとって、アルコールは単なる飲み物以上に、しばしば人と交流する為の大切なツールにもなります。「飲み会」の慣習についても紹介しましょう。

photo：ちよし / PIXTA（ピクスタ）

アルコール―Facts

- 酒の年間消費量　(annual consumption of sake)―90ℓ/人
- 酒蔵の多い県 (top 3 pref. holding sake breweries)
  ―①新潟県 (Niigata)　②長野県 (Nagano)　③兵庫県 (Hyogo)

参照：国税庁「平成２９年度清酒製造業の概況」「平成３０年酒のしおり」

① The Unique Drinking
日本独自の飲酒文化

68

In Japan, drinking is about not only enjoying the taste of alcoholic beverages but also building and maintaining good relationships with others.

 日本では、お酒を飲むことはアルコール飲料の味を楽しむだけではなく、人間関係を築き維持することを意味します。

☐alcoholic beverages
アルコール飲料

For example, drinking with colleagues and bosses is regarded as an important activity at workplace, although the younger generations' lifestyle is changing from the previous generations.

 若い世代のライフスタイルは前の世代から変化しているものの、職場で同僚や上司とお酒を飲むことは大事なこととされています。

☐colleague 名 同僚
☐is regarded as
〜とされている
☐previous 形 前の

② Some rules to remember
覚えておきたいルール

When you drink with others, the first round that everyone tends to order is beer. Once ordering is done, wait until everyone gets a drink. When all the drinks are served, say *kampai* to toast. While you are drinking, it is customary to pour drinks for others around you, in particular for someone above you socially like your boss.

- □ first round　1回目
- □ tend to
　　～の傾向にある
- □ toast 動 乾杯する
- □ customary
　　形 慣習で

訳 ▶ 人とお酒を飲む際には、皆まず始めの飲み物としてビールを頼むことが一般的です。注文が済んだら、全員に飲み物が出されるまで待ちましょう。全ての飲み物が出されたら、カンパイと言って乾杯します。飲んでいる最中は、特に上司など社会的に上になる人に、お酒を注ぐのが慣習です。

③ Various drinking occasions
多彩にあるお酒の機会

The general term for gatherings over alcohol is called *nomikai*. *Shinnenkai* is a gathering for the New Year celebration. *Bonenkai* is the end of the year party to forget about anything bad that has happened during the year.

- □ gathering
　　名 集まり

訳 ▶ お酒を囲んだ集まりを通常、飲み会と言います。新年会は新年を祝う会です。忘年会は一年の終わりに、その年にあった嫌なことを忘れるためのパーティーです。

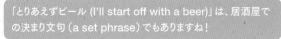

「とりあえずビール (I'll start off with a beer)」は、居酒屋での決まり文句（a set phrase）でもありますね！

飲み物② 日本のアルコール
Alcohol Beverages of Japan

🍚 105kcal

メニュー
54

日本酒
Sake

photo：イグのマスタ / PIXTA（ピクスタ）

料理のキーワード

食材	rice（米）, *koji* mold（麹菌）, yeast（イースト）, alcohol（アルコール）, whole grain（玄米）
調理法	mill（挽く）, polish（磨く）, ferment（発酵する）, brew（醸造する）, heat（温める）
調理器具・器	*sake* bottle（徳利）, small *sake* cup（お猪口）, large *sake* cup（ぐい呑み）
味わい	aromatic（香り高い）, fruity（フルーティーな）, dry（辛口）, refreshing（すっきりとした）, soft（軽い）, rounded（まろやか）

150

説明してみよう！

69

1 Japanese *sake* is pronounced not as "saki", but saké. It is brewed by fermenting rice with water, *koji* mold and yeast. *Sake* has around 15% alcohol, which is slightly higher than wine. Many breweries have made *sake* for generations with pride and craftsmanship.

訳 日本酒は「サキ」ではなく「サケ」と発音します。米、水、麹と酵母を発酵させて醸造するものです。日本酒はワインより少し高めの約15%のアルコール度数です。多くの酒蔵が何世代にもわたり、誇りと熟練仕事で日本酒を作ってきました。

- □ be pronounced as ～と発音される
- □ brew 動 醸造する
- □ slightly 副 少し
- □ brewery 名 醸造所
- □ craftsmanship 名 熟練仕事

2 *Sake* is categorized into different types by the milling rates of rice and production methods. For example, *ginjo* is made with rice that was polished down to 60% of the whole grains and added alcohol. It is highly aromatic and fruity.

訳 日本酒の種類は精米歩合と製造方法により区分されます。例えば吟醸は、玄米をその60%まで磨き落としたもので、アルコールを加えています。非常に香りが高くフルーティな味がします。

- □ milling rates of rice 精米歩合（白米の割合）
- □ polish 動 ～をみがく
- □ whole grain 玄米

3 *Honjozo* is made with rice milled down to 70%. It has a dry and refreshing taste. The soft and rounded flavor of *sake* goes well with various dishes, including western-style dishes.

訳 本醸造は70%まで磨いた米で作ります。辛口でさっぱりしています。柔らかく丸みのある日本酒の風味は、洋風の料理を含め多彩な料理と合います。

- □ dry 形 辛口の
- □ go well with ～と合う

151

日本のアルコール
Alcohol Beverages of Japan

150kcal

メニュー
55

焼酎
Shochu

photo: jazzman / PIXTA (ピクスタ)

料理のキーワード

 食材
potato (芋), barley (麦), rice (米), cold water (冷水),
hot water (温かい水), fruit juice (果汁), syrup (シロップ),
sparkling water (炭酸水)

 調理法
distill (蒸留する), straight (ストレート), on the rocks (ロック), mix (混ぜる)

 味わい
delicate aroma (繊細な香り)

説明してみよう！

70

1 *Shochu* is as popular as *sake* in Japan. It is made by distilling a wide variety of ingredients, such as potato (*imo*), barley (*mugi*) and rice (*kome*). Because premium *shochu* (*otsurui*) is distilled only once, you can enjoy the delicate aroma of the ingredients.

□distill 動 蒸留する
□barley 名 大麦

訳 日本で焼酎は、日本酒と同様に人気です。芋、麦、米など、様々な原料を蒸留して作ります。特級の焼酎（乙類）は一度しか蒸留しないため、原料の繊細な風味を味わうことができます。

Shochu generally has 20-25% alcohol. The majority of premium *shochu* is made in Kyushu. *Awamori* from *Okinawa* is similar to *shochu* but the ingredients and production methods are slightly different.

□majority 名 大多数

訳 焼酎のアルコールは20-25%程度です。良質の焼酎の多くは九州で作られます。沖縄産の泡盛は焼酎に近いですが、原料と製法は多少異なります。

2 Premium *shochu* is often served straight, on the rocks, *mizuwari* (mixed with cold water) and *oyuwari* (mixed with hot water). *Chuhai* (*shochu* highball) is a very popular way to drink non-premium *shochu*. It is *shochu* mixed with fruit juice or syrup and sparkling water.

□straight
形 ストレート
□syrup 名 シロップ
□sparkling water
炭酸水

訳 良質の焼酎はよくストレート、ロック、水割り、お湯割りで飲まれます。酎ハイ（焼酎ハイボール）は非常に人気の高い、特級以外の焼酎の飲み方です。これは焼酎を炭酸水、果汁やシロップで混ぜたものです。

梅酒 **155**kcal / ビール **40**kcal

メニュー 56 その他の種類の日本のお酒
Other Types of Japanese Alcohol

photo：CORA / PIXTA (ピクスタ)

説明してみよう！

 71

---

1 *Umeshu* is a traditional liqueur made by steeping tart Japanese plums, rock ice and *shochu*. It is sweet and has 10-15% alcohol. You can enjoy it straight, mixed with tea, or make sweets with it.

訳 梅酒は伝統的な、酸味の高い梅と氷砂糖、焼酎を漬けたリキュールです。甘い味で10-15%のアルコール度数を持ちます。ストレート、お茶と混ぜる、お菓子の素材に使うなどの形で楽しめます。

□liqueur
　名 リキュール

□steep 　動 浸す

□tart 　形 すっぱい

154

2 Japanese whisky is drawing a huge attention worldwide lately. It is based on the style of Scotch whisky, but it is generally more delicate and less smoky.

□ drawing a huge attention
注目を集める
□ smoky
形 燻し香のある

訳▶日本のウイスキーは最近世界的に注目を浴びています。スコッチのスタイルを基本にしていますが、大半のものはより味わいが繊細で、燻し香が穏やかです。

3 The majority of Japanese beer has been lager-style. However, since 1994 when the tax law changed to allow smaller-size production of beer, many craft beer breweries were born. Now you can find more variety of beer in Japan.

□ lager
名 ラガービール
□ brewery 名 醸造所

訳▶日本のビールの大半はラガー系でしたが、1994年に税法が変わって小規模でビールが生産できるようになり、多くのクラフトビールの醸造所が生まれました。今では日本に多彩なビールが見られます。

4 Japanese wine is becoming popular in recent years. The most well-known grape is *Koshu*. This white variety has elegant acidity and aroma of citrus and peach.

□ variety 名 品種
□ elegant 形 優美な
□ acidity 名 酸味

訳▶日本産ワインは近年人気を高めています。代表的なぶどうの品種は甲州。この白ワイン品種は優美な酸味と柑橘類や桃の香りを持っています。

日本のカクテル文化
Japanese Cocktail Culture

カクテルは米国や欧州で何世紀もの歴史を持ちますが、日本人がカクテルを飲み始めたのは20世紀初頭に過ぎません。日本のカクテルバーは通常クラシック系カクテルの芸術性とバーテンダーのおもてなしを静かに楽しむ場所です。これは活気があり、バーテンダーが一杯のグラスに創意を込める米国のカクテルバーと大きく異なります。

日本のカクテル文化は独自性が高く、海外で高く評価されています。日本のバーテンダーは、シェーカーの振り方から混ぜ方、提供の仕方まで、型とブレのなさを重視します。外国人は日本人のバーテンダーが手で氷を削るのに驚きます。海外からバーテンダーが日本を訪れる際には、よく日本製の優れたバー用品を買い求めます。

Although cocktails have centuries of history in the US and Europe, the Japanese started to drink them only in the early 20th century. Cocktail bars in Japan are generally the place to enjoy the art of classic-based cocktail and the hospitality of bartenders quietly. This is very different from most American cocktail bars where the ambiance is lively and bartenders showcase their creativity in a glass.

The Japanese cocktail culture is unique and well-respected abroad. Japanese bartenders emphasize rituals and precision in making cocktails from shaking, stirring to serving. Foreigners are surprised to know that Japanese bartenders even hand-carved ice for a perfect glass of cocktail. When bartenders from abroad visit Japan, they often purchase well-designed Japanese barware.

4章

和菓子

Japanese Sweets

和菓子
Japanese Sweets

ここでは定番の和菓子を通して、洋菓子とはつくり方や材料の異なる特徴や、季節を彩るものとしての和菓子について紹介してみましょう。

和菓子—Facts

- 消費額全国平均 (annual average expenditure) — ¥3,444／人 (person)
- 最も和菓子を食べる県 (prefectures most consume *wagashi*) —
  ①石川 (Ishikawa)　②岐阜 (Gifu)　③滋賀 (Shiga)

参照：総務省「家計調査（2016年〜2018年平均）」

① Sweets to enjoy with green tea
日本茶と楽しむ菓子　⬇72

There are some major events in the history of *wagashi*. First, tea was introduced to Japan from China in the early 12th century, and *wagashi* became a part of tea ceremony over time.

 和菓子の歴史にはいくつかの大きな出来事があります。まず12世紀に中国からお茶が導入され、やがて和菓子は茶道の一部となります。

In the 16th century, the Portuguese sugary sweets inspired the production of *wagashi* made with added sugar. During the Edo period, *wagashi* became more widely available to the public due to the increase of sugar imports.

 16世紀ポルトガルの甘いお菓子が、砂糖を加えた和菓子の生産に導きます。江戸時代には砂糖の輸入量が増し、和菓子が一般市民の間で広く楽しまれるようになりました。

□over time　やがて

□sugary
　形 砂糖を含んだ
□inspire
　動 ひらめきをあたえる
□due to　〜が原因で

② Difference from *yogashi* (Western sweets)
洋菓子との区別

Unlike *yogashi* animal-based ingredients like dairy and eggs are not used to make *wagashi*. As a result, *wagashi* tends to be less fatty. On the other hand, *wagashi* often contains a lot of sugar. Also, *wagashi* is made by a variety of cooking methods beyond baking, such as steaming, kneading and molding.

□ animal-based
 動物性の
□ dairy 名 乳製品
□ contain 動 含む
□ knead 動 練る
□ mold 動 型に入れる

 洋菓子と違い、和菓子は乳製品や卵などの動物性食材を使いません。そのため和菓子は脂肪分が少なめです。一方和菓子は多くの砂糖を含んでいます。また和菓子には、焼く以上に蒸す、練って型に入れるなど多彩な製法があります。

③ Reflection of seasons
季節を映しだすもの

Wagashi is highly seasonal. Although many types of *wagashi* are available throughout the year, you can find unique *wagashi* items for each season.
For example, pink colored *wagashi* is common in spring to represent the cherry blossom season. *Wagashi* with the shape and colors of autumn leaves are another popular item.

□ throughout the
 year 一年中
□ colored ～色の
□ autumn leaves
 紅葉

 和菓子は季節性が高いものです。多くの和菓子は年中販売されていますが、季節ごとに独自の品が見つかります。例えば桜の季節を代表するピンク色の和菓子は春に目立ちます。紅葉の色と形を持った和菓子も人気です。

ポルトガル人の日本来航まで (until the Portuguese arrived in Japan)、和菓子は砂糖を使わず自然素材から甘さを得ていました (wagashi were naturally sweetened without sugar)！

和菓子
Japanese Sweets

235kcal | ¥〜300

メニュー
58

餅菓子
Mochi gashi / Mochi Sweets

photo：grace / PIXTA（ピクスタ）

料理のキーワード

食材
adzuki bean paste（あんこ）, *mochi* dough（もち生地）, cornstarch（コーンスターチ）, salt-cured cherry leaf（桜の葉の塩漬け）, oak leaf（柏の葉）

調理法
stuff with（詰める）, wrap with（包む）, dust with（まぶす）, mash（つぶす）

味わい
sweet（甘い）, soft（柔らかい）, fluffy（ふわふわした）

160

説明してみよう!

1 There are many types of *wagashi* made with *mochi*. *Daifuku* is a *mochi* filled with *anko*, or sweet *adzuki* bean paste. Because the soft and fluffy dough is dusted with cornstarch, it does not stick to your hand and has a unique mouth feel.

□ fill with 〜をつめる
□ fluffy 形 ふわふわの
□ dough 名 生地
□ dust with 〜まぶす
□ stick to 〜にくっつく

訳 餅で作る和菓子はたくさんあります。大福はあんこを詰めた餅です。柔らかくふわふわした生地にはコーンスターチをまぶしてあるので手にベタベタつかず、独特の食感もあります。

Sakura mochi is a pink-colored *mochi* stuffed with *anko* and wrapped with salt-cured *sakura* (cherry) leaves. It is eaten during the cherry blossom season in particular on *Hina matsuri* (Girl's Day on March 3rd).

□ wrap with 〜で包む
□ salt-cured 塩漬けの

訳 桜餅はピンク色の餅で、あんこを詰めて桜の葉の塩漬けで包んであります。ことにひな祭り（3月3日の女の子のお祭り）など、桜の花の季節に食べます。

2 *Ohagi* or *botamochi* is another *wagashi* made with *mochi* and *anko*. But unlike *daifuku*, *anko* is the wrapping and *mochi* is the filling. Also, the rice is mashed half way to make *mochi* that it has a different texture from regular *mochi*.

□ filling 名 詰めもの
□ mush half way 半ごろし

訳 おはぎ（ぼた餅）も餅とあんこで作る和菓子です。しかし大福とは違い、餅があんこの中に入っています。また、もち米はつぶしきっていない（半ごろし）ので、通常の餅と違った食感があります。

 195kcal  ¥〜200

団子
Dango / Rice Dumplings

photo：wasaitax / PIXTA（ピクスタ）

料理のキーワード

 食材

dumpling（団子）, rice flour dough（米粉生地）, *yomogi* herb（よもぎ）, soy flour（黄粉）, sweet soy sauce（みたらし）, *adzuki* bean（小豆）

 調理法

knead（生地をこねる）, coat with（覆う）

 調理器具・器

bamboo skewer（竹串）

 味わい

aromatic（香り高い）, sweet（甘い）, toasty（香ばしい）

説明してみよう!

74

1 *Dango* are small boiled dumplings made of rice flour. They are often served on bamboo skewers.

訳 団子は米粉の小さな玉を茹でたものです。多くの場合竹串に刺して出されます。

□skewer 名 串

2 *Mitarashi dango* are coated with a sauce made with soy sauce and sugar. *Yomogi dango* are beautiful green, since aromatic herb *yomogi* is mixed in the dough. *Kinako dango* are dusted with sweet and toasty soy flour. *Oshiruko* is a bowl of *dango* and sweet red bean soup.

訳 みたらし団子は醤油と砂糖のソースがからめてあります。よもぎ団子は、風味豊かな香草、よもぎが生地に織り込まれているので美しい緑色をしています。きな粉団子は甘く香ばしい大豆の粉をまぶしてあります。おしるこは甘い小豆のスープと団子を碗に入れたものです。

□dough 名 生地
□dust with
  ～をまぶす
□toasty 形 香ばしい
□flour 名 粉

3 *Dango* are also served at special occasions. For instance, *tsukimi dango* are eaten on the night of the full moon in fall to celebrate the harvest. *Dango* are plated in the shape of pyramid and put in a place where you can enjoy the full moon in the background.

訳 団子は特別な機会にも出されます。例えば月見団子は、収穫を祝って満月の夜に食べます。団子はピラミッド型に皿に盛り、背景に月を眺めて楽しめる場所に置きます。

□full moon 満月
□harvest 名 収穫
□pyramid
  名 ピラミッド
□put in ～に置く

和菓子
Japanese Sweets

 260kcal  ¥〜200

メニュー
60

饅頭
Manju / Sweet Bun with Adzuki Bean Paste

photo：ささざわ / PIXTA（ピクスタ）

料理のキーワード

 食材
adzuki bean paste（あんこ）, white kidney bean（白いんげん豆）, flour dough（小麦粉の生地）, chestnut（栗）, yeast（酵母）, *koji* mold（麹菌）

 調理法
stuff with（詰める）, wrap（包む）, steam（蒸す）/ bake（焼く）

 味わい
sweet（甘い）, aromatic（香り高い）

164

説明してみよう！

75

1 *Manju* is a type of *wagashi* typically stuffed with *anko*, or sweet *adzuki* bean paste.   Unlike *mochi* sweets, it is made with flour and steamed or baked.

> **訳** 饅頭とは一般にあんこを詰めた和菓子です。餅菓子と違い、小麦粉で作られ蒸すか焼きます。

2 An example of steamed *manju* is *saka manju*. It is *anko* wrapped inside special dough. Yeast and *koji* mold are added to the dough. These are also the ingredients of Japanese *sake*. That is why it has an aroma of *sake*.

> **訳** 蒸し饅頭の例には酒饅頭があります。あんこを特殊な生地に包んであります。酵母と麹を生地に加えてあります。これらは日本酒の材料でもあります。酒饅頭は日本酒の香りがするのはこのためです。

□ yeast　**名** 酵母

3 *Ningyo yaki* is a baked *manju* filled with *anko*. *Ningyo* means a doll. *Ningyo yaki* can be shaped differently from Japanese ancient gods to Hello Kitty. *Kuri manju* is a baked *manju* that looks like chestnut. Inside is *shiroan*, which is a sweet bean paste made with white kidney beans.

> **訳** 人形焼はあんこが詰まった焼き饅頭です。「ニンギョウ」とは人形のことです。人形焼には日本の古代の神様からハローキティまで、様々な形があります。栗饅頭は栗に似せて焼いた饅頭です。中身は白いんげん豆で作る甘いペーストです。

□ differently　**副** 様々な
□ ancient　**形** 古代の
□ chestnut　**名** 栗
□ white kidney bean　白いんげん豆

和菓子
Japanese Sweets

鯛焼き 230kcal ¥～200

メニュー 61 鯛焼き、どら焼き、最中
Taiyaki , Dorayaki & Monaka

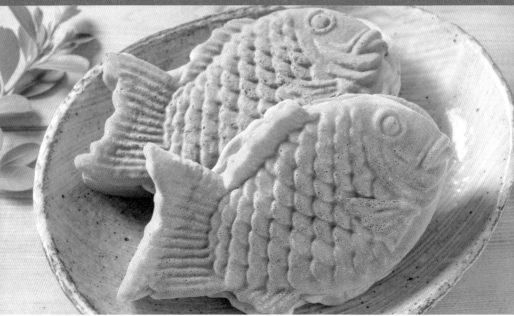

photo：my room / PIXTA（ピクスタ）

料理のキーワード

 食材
pancake（パンケーキ）, rice flour wafer（米粉のウエハース）, *adzuki* bean paste（あんこ）, custard cream（カスタードクリーム）, chestnut（栗）, ice cream（アイスクリーム）

 調理法
pack（詰める）, bake（焼く）, sandwich（挟む）

 調理器具・器
mold（型）

 味わい
fluffy（ふわふわした）/ thin（薄い）, crispy（パリッとした）, airy（軽い）

166

説明してみよう!

76

1 *Taiyaki* is a type of *manju*. It has a unique shape of *tai* fish (sea bream). It is so popular that you can find it at *ennichi*, which are traditional festivals held at shrines, temples.

訳 鯛焼きは饅頭の一種です。独特の鯛の形をしています。とても人気が高いため、神社やお寺で開かれる伝統的なお祭り、縁日でも見られます。

Another popular manju is dorayaki. Anko is sandwiched between small pancakes. It is also the favorite food of the Japanese anime character *Doraemon*.

訳 どら焼きも人気の饅頭です。あんこは小さなパンケーキに挟まれています。日本のアニメのキャラクター、ドラえもんの好物でもあります。

2 *Monaka* is *anko* packed inside a thin wafer. The dough is made with rice flour and baked in a mold. The crispy, airy dough enhances the taste of the filling. The filling can be *koshi an* (regular smooth *anko*), *tsubu an* (*anko* made with partially crushed *adzuki* beans), or even ice cream nowadays.

訳 最中は薄いウエハースにあんこを包んだものです。生地を米粉で作り、型に入れて焼きます。パリッと軽い生地が中身の味を引き立てます。中身にはこしあん（普通の滑らかなあんこ）、つぶあん（小豆を半分潰したあんこ）、あるいは最近ではアイスクリームなどもあります。

□ sea bream　鯛
□ shrine　名 神社
□ sandwich between
　〜に挟む

□ wafer
　名 ウエハース
□ mold　名 型
□ smooth
　形 なめらかな
□ airy　形 軽い
□ enhance　動 高める
□ partially crushed
　部分的に潰された

和菓子
Japanese Sweets

メニュー **62**

日本のクラッカーとキャンディ
Japanese Crackers & Candy

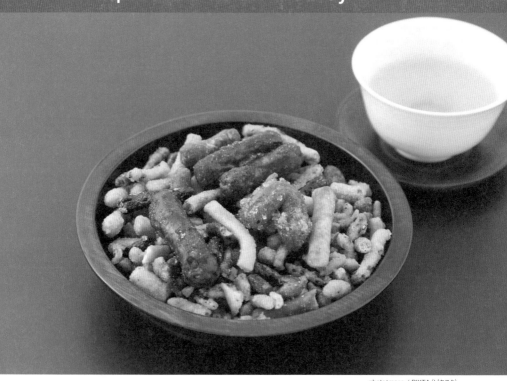

photo：masa / PIXTA（ピクスタ）

料理のキーワード

 rice（米）,sticky rice（もち米）/ flour（小麦粉）, yeast（イースト）, brown sugar（黒糖）/ sugar（砂糖）, syrup（シロップ）

 bake（焼く）/deep-fry（揚げる）/coat（表面を覆う）,crystallize（結晶化させる）

 salty（塩味のある）, sweet（甘い）, rich（深みのある）

168

1 *Senbei* are baked rice crackers. They are typically flavored with soy sauce or salt. There are *senbei* made with sticky rice. Larger ones are called *okaki* and smaller ones are *arare*.

> 訳 煎餅は焼いた米のクラッカーです。通常醤油か塩で味付けされています。もち米で作る煎餅もあります。大きなものはおかき、小さなものはあられです。

□cracker
名 クラッカー
□sticky rice　もち米

2 *Karinto* are classic deep-fried sweet crackers made with flour, yeast and brown sugar. They have a distinctive deep rich taste from brown sugar.

> 訳 かりんとうは小麦粉、イーストと黒糖で作る、伝統的な甘い揚げたクラッカーです。黒糖独特の深く濃厚な味わいです。

□yeast　名 イースト
□brown sugar　黒糖
□distinctive
形 濃厚な

3 *Kompeito* is a star-shaped tiny colorful sugar candy. It originated in the candy brought to Japan by the Portuguese in the 16th century. It takes one to two weeks to make *kompeito*, because skilled craftsmen slowly and repeatedly coat the sugar at the core with syrup and crystalize it to make the star shape.

> 訳 金平糖は星型の小さな砂糖菓子です。16世紀にポルトガル人がもたらした飴が起源です。職人がゆっくりと繰り返し、核になる砂糖にシロップをからめながら結晶させて星型にするため、生産には一、二週間かかります。

□tiny　形 小さい
□originate in
　～に起源がある
□coat　動 表面を覆う
□core　名 核
□crystalize
動 結晶化させる

茶道と和菓子
Wagashi and Tea Ceremony

外国人はよく、彩り豊かで繊細な和菓子を芸術だといいます。和菓子は茶道と共に発展しました。茶道の目的はお客が最高の時間を過ごすことにあります。だから亭主がはっとするように美しい、季節感豊かな和菓子をお客に提供するのです。

茶道で和菓子はお茶の前に出されます。理由はお客の口に残った和菓子の甘みが、苦い抹茶の味を引き立てるからです。また和菓子は、お茶のカフェインが空っぽの胃を痛めるリスクを軽減してくれます。和菓子はよく菓銘という特別な名前を持っています。お菓子に伴う想像を掻き立てるものです。菓銘は俳句や自然など様々なものから来ています。

Foreigners often describe colorful and delicate wagashi as art. Wagashi was developed along with the Japanese tea ceremony. The purpose of tea ceremony is to create the most enjoyable experience for the guests. That is why the host offers beautiful seasonal wagashi to the guests.

Wagashi is served before tea at a tea ceremony. The reason is the remaining sweetness of wagashi in the guests' mouth complements the taste of bitter matcha green tea. Also, wagashi mitigates the potential damage from tea's caffeine to the guests' empty stomach. Wagashi often has a specific name called *kamei*. It triggers imagination associated with the sweet. *Kamei* comes from various sources such as classic haiku and nature.

5章

さまざまな
和食のスタイル

Various Styles of
Washoku

日本の弁当文化
Japanese *Bento* Culture

世界でも有名になった日本の弁当。日常から特別な行事まで活躍し、単なる持ち運びできる食事以上の意味をもつ弁当文化を紹介してみましょう。

photo：Graphs / PIXTA（ピクスタ）

弁当―Facts

- 定番のおかず (popular side dishes of bento) ―
  ①玉子焼き（omlet）　②から揚げ (*karaage*)　③ウインナー (Wienerwurst)
- 駅弁の種類 (the number of *ekiben* varieties) ― 2,000 以上 (more than 2,000)

参照：マルハニチロ調べ

① *Bento* is more than a portable meal
弁当は携帯食のみならず
⬇78

Bento is an essential element of Japanese culture. You can find colorful and nutritious foods packed neatly in a *bento* box everywhere in Japan from convenience stores, train stations to theaters. Homemade *bento* is important for school children and office workers.

 弁当は単に持ち運びできる食事のことです。しかし日本文化に欠かせない要素の一つとなっています。日本ではコンビニから駅、劇場まであらゆる場所で、色とりどりの栄養豊かな食べ物が、きっちり詰まった弁当箱を見つけることができます。自家製弁当は学校に通う子供にも会社員にも大切なものです。

□neatly　副 きっちりと
□homemade
　形 自家製の

Bento is also a centerpiece of seasonal events such as cherry blossom viewing parties.

訳 弁当はお花見などの季節行事の要にもなっています。

□centerpiece
　名 最も大切なもの

172

② The role of Japonica rice
ジャポニカ米の役割

They say a reason why *bento* became so popular in Japan is that sticky Japonica rice stays moist and delicious than other types of rice such as Indica.

訳 日本で弁当がとても人気になった理由の一つは、水分が多く粘り気のあるジャポニカ米は、インディカなど多種の米に比べ、美味しさがより長く保たれるからとも言われます。

 ③ Bento can be fancy
高級な弁当も

Bento can be very elaborate. For example, *shokado bento* is created by a *kaiseki* chef in Kyoto in the early 20th century.

□elaborate
　形 手の込んだ

訳 弁当はとても手の込んだ高級なものにもなり得ます。例えば松花堂弁当は、20世紀初めに京都の会席シェフが考案したものです。

The bento box is divided into four compartments to separate tastes of each section. They say the divided structure of the box came from the container that was used by farmers to store seeds in 16th century.

□compartment
　名 仕切り
□container
　名 入れ物

訳 弁当箱はそれぞれの味が混じらないよう四つに仕切られています。仕切りのついた構造は、16世紀に農民が種をしまっておくのに使っていた入れ物から来ていると言われます。

仕出しと呼ばれる事前予約の弁当（pre-ordered bento called shidashi）は、結婚式など様々な機会で一般的です（popular for various occasions such as weddings）！

173

🍚 500~900kcal/個　👛 ¥～1,000

メニュー
64

幕の内弁当
Makunouchi bento / Classic *Bento*

photo：june. / PIXTA（ピクスタ）

料理のキーワード

rice ball（おにぎり）, black sesame seed（黒ごま）, pickled red plum（梅干し）, rolled omelet（出汁巻き玉子）, grilled fish（焼き魚）, deep-fried seafood（魚介の揚げ物）, meatball（ミートボール）, cutlet（カツ）, simmered vegetables（野菜の煮物）, steamed caked of minced fish（かまぼこ）, pickles（漬物）, simmered side dish flavored with soy sauce（佃煮）

put~ in a bento box（弁当箱に～を詰める）

説明してみよう！

79

1 *Makunouchi bento* is probably the most classic *bento*. It was born as a meal eaten at theaters between acts during the Edo period. It contains well-balanced nutritious food.

> 訳▶幕の内弁当は最も代表的な弁当と言えるでしょう。江戸時代、芝居の幕間に食べる食事として生まれました。栄養のバランスのとれた食べ物が詰められています。

□act 名 芝居
□well-balanced
　バランスのとれた

2 There are always small cylinder rice balls sprinkled with black sesame seeds in *makunouchi*. Pickled red plum may be on the rice balls to kill unwanted bacteria.

> 訳▶幕内には必ず黒ゴマを散らした小さな俵形のおにぎりが入っています。雑菌を殺すためによく梅干しがのっています。

□cylinder 名 俵
□sprinkle with
　〜を散らす
□pickled red plum
　梅干し
□unwanted bacteria
　雑菌

3 Like many other *bento*, *makunouchi bento* is made based on *washoku*'s important principle "*gomi goshoku goho*" (p16). The variation of taste, texture and colors make a *bento* delicious, enjoyable, satisfying and healthy.

> 訳▶他の弁当同様、幕内弁当は和食の重要な原則「五味五色五法」(p16) にならって作られています。味、食感、色彩の多様さが、弁当を美味しく、楽しく、満足感のある健康的なものにしてくれます。

駅弁 *Ekiben* / Railway *Bento*

Ekiben is a *bento* that represents the regional food culture.
It is sold at *eki* (train stations), onboard train carts and local shops.
駅弁は地方の食文化を代表する弁当です。駅や、列車内、地元の店で購入できます。

① photo：株式会社荻野屋

② photo：株式会社　南洋軒

③ photo：株式会社番匠本店

説明してみよう！

80

① 峠の釜めし *Toge no Kamameshi*

This *bento* started to sell in Gunma in 1958. The small ceramic pot contains rice, chicken, *shiitake* mushroom, burdock roots, quail egg, chestnut, apricot and red pickled ginger. The pot comes from the famous pottery region *mashiko*.

訳 峠の釜めしは1958年群馬県で発売されました。小さな陶器の釜には、米、鶏肉、椎茸、ごぼう、うずらの卵、栗、杏、紅生姜が入っています。釜は有名な陶器の産地益子産です。

□ burdock root
ごぼう

□ quail 名 うずら

□ red pickled ginger
紅しょうが

□ pottery 名 陶器

② 越前かにめし *Echizen Kanimeshi*

This *bento* was created in Fukui Prefecture in 1961. The area is famous as a fishing base for crabs. The bottom of the *bento* box is rice cooked with flavorful snow crabmeats. It is topped with more snow and red snow crabmeats.

訳 越前かにめしは1961年福井県で生まれました。この地域はカニの漁港として知られます。弁当箱の底は風味豊かなズワイガニの身と一緒に炊いたご飯です。その上にズワイガニと紅ズワイガニの肉が盛られています。

□ fishing base 漁場

□ snow crabmeat
ズワイガニの身

□ red snow crabmeats
紅ズワイガニの身

③ 近江牛すき焼き弁当 *Ohmi* Beef *Sukiyaki Bento*

The theme of the *bento* is the highly marbled *wagyu* beef from Shiga The thinly sliced beef is simmered with soy sauce, sugar, Japanese green onion, baked *tofu*, egg, mushroom and other vegetables.

訳 この弁当のテーマはサシがしっかり入った滋賀県産の和牛です。薄切りの牛肉は醤油、砂糖、ねぎ、焼き豆腐、卵、キノコなどと一緒に煮てあります。

□ marbled
形 サシの入った

177

日本の弁当箱の独自のデザイン
The Unique Design of Japanese Bento Boxes

海外でも職場や学校に弁当を持っていくのは一般的ですが、日本の弁当よりカジュアルです。例えばビニール袋に入れたシンプルなハムとチーズのサンドイッチはアメリカでの定番ランチです。

特別な弁当箱も日本独自です。豪華な漆塗りの重箱は、すでに江戸時代、上流階級の花見などの特別な機会によく使われていました。曲げわっぱは美しい木製の弁当箱です。蒸した良質の杉やヒノキを入念に手で曲げ、本体と蓋が完璧にはまるようにします。快い木の香りが中の食べ物に移ります。また木が水分を吸収するため、食べ物の鮮度がより保たれます。

Many people bring lunch to work or school around the world, but the Japanese bento is more complex. For example, a simple ham and cheese sandwich in a plastic bag would be a standard lunch in the U.S.

Special *bento* boxes are unique to Japan too. Fancy multi-tiered lacquered *bento* boxes were already popular during the Edo period among the nobles for special occasions such as a cherry blossom viewing party.   *Magewappa* is a beautiful wooden *bento* box. It is made by steaming high-quality cedar or Japanese cypress and carefully bending it by hand to perfectly fit the body and lid of the box. The pleasant aroma of the wood is transferred to the food inside. Also, food stays fresher because the wood absorbs the moisture of food.

キャラ弁
Character Bento

キャラクター弁当、もしくはキャラ弁とは、パンダ、トトロ、ピカチュウなどの動物、アニメや漫画のキャラクター、その他可愛いイメージをテーマにした弁当です。外国人はその精巧さにとても感心します。もともとこれらのキャラクターは、子供が弁当を食べたくなることを狙って取り入れられたものです。近年 SNS への写真の投稿が盛んになり、キャラ弁人気に拍車をかけました。

作る側にとって、子供が喜ぶ手の込んだキャラ弁は大仕事です。そのため、ご飯用の動物の形をした型、海苔の穴あけ機など、たくさんの道具が存在しています。またオンラインでは可愛いキャラ弁の作り方のコツがたくさん見つかります。

Character *bento*, or *charaben*, is a *bento* box that features animals, characters from anime, manga or other cute images, such as panda, Totoro and Pikachu. Foreigners are highly impressed with how elaborately made they are. Originally these characters were introduced to *bento* to induce kids to eat their lunch. The prosperity of social media such as photo posting boosted the popularity of *charaben* in recent years.

It is a lot of work for cooks to make a detailed *charaben* that children would like. As a result, there are many tools available to help them, such as animal-shaped molds for rice, seaweed hole punches, and eyeball-shaped picks. Also, tips to make a cute *charaben* is widely available online.

行事食
Festive Fare

祝日や伝統的な行事にあわせて食べられる行事食には、健康や幸運への願いが込められています。それぞれの料理に込められた意味を紹介しましょう。

photo：hattori / PIXTA（ピクスタ）

行事食—Facts

- 5つの重要な行事（五節句）(5 most important seasonal festival)—
  1/7 七草の節句 (the seven herbs festival)、3/3 桃の節句 (Girls' festival)、
  5/5 端午の節句 (Boys' Festival)、7/7 七夕の節句 (Tanabata)、
  9/9 菊の節句 (the chrysanthemum festival)

① Food for special occasions
特別な機会の食べ物

81

Traditional observances and holidays are often associated with specific fare in Japan. These celebratory foods are made to keep good health and invite good fortune.

 日本の伝統的なしきたりや祝日には、よく特別な食べ物が伴います。こうした祝いの食べ物は健康の維持や幸運を招くよう作られています。

For example, *nanakusa gayu* is eaten on January 7th to stay healthy for the rest of the year. *Nanakusa* means seven herbs. Young leaves of the herbs are cooked with rice and made into porridge. It is a highly nutritious seasonal dish.

 たとえば七草がゆは、その先一年を健康に過ごせるよう1月7日に食べます。七草は、7種の薬草のことです。これらの薬草の若葉は米と一緒に調理し、おかゆにします。とても栄養価の高い旬の料理です。

□ associate with
〜を伴う
□ observance
名 しきたり
□ fare 名 食事

□ porridge 名 おかゆ

Expelling evil spirits
邪気を払う

Some foods have spiritual meanings. For instance, there is a ritual called *setsubun* on February 3rd. In order to drive away evil spirits, people throw roasted soybeans around their houses, shrines or temples. After the event, you have to pick up the number of beans that corresponds to your age.

□ritual 名 しきたり
□drive away
　〜を払う
□correspond to
　〜に相当する

訳▶ 霊に関する意味合いのある料理もあります。たとえば2月3日には節分というしきたりがあります。邪気を払うため、炒った大豆を家、神社、お寺などの中に撒きます。終わったら自分の年齢の数の豆を食べなくてはいけません。

 ## Connecting with ancestors
祖先との繋がり

Obon is an important event to honor the spirits of ancestors. It is held around August 15th for a few days. During the period, people offer flowers, fruits and sweets to ancestors and eat *shojin ryori*, which is the vegan cuisine that was developed by Buddhist monks. Also, *Bon odori* dancing festivals are held where you can find traditional street foods.

□honor
　動 〜をあがめる
□ancestor 名 祖先
□vegan
　形 菜食主義の
□monk 名 僧

訳▶ お盆は祖先の霊をあがめる重要な行事です。8月15日前後に数日間に渡って行われます。その期間は祖先に花、果物、お菓子を供え、仏教僧が生み出したヴィーガン料理、精進料理を食べます。また伝統的な露店が並ぶ盆踊りも開催されます。

七草は、セリ(water dropwort)、ナズナ(shepherd's purse)、ゴギョウ(cudweed)、ハコベラ(chickweed)、ホトケノザ(henbit)、スズナ(tunip)、スズシロ(*daikon* raddish)です！

181

メニュー 68 年越しそば
Toshikoshi soba / New Year's Eve noodles

photo：jazzman / PIXTA(ピクスタ)

photo：Ziyuuichi Tomowo / PIXTA(ピクスタ)

photo：jazzman / PIXTA(ピクスタ)

説明してみよう！

1 In Japan, the biggest event of the year is the New Year. It is customary for the Japanese to clean up the entire house before the end of the year, so that they are prepared to welcome the New Year with a fresh mind.

訳 日本では一年最大のイベントは新年です。気持ちを切り替えて新年を迎えることができるよう、年が終わる前に家中掃除をする習慣があります。

The New Year's Eve is a sacred evening to let go of the old year and embrace the arrival of the coming year.

訳 大晦日は、古い一年を手放し、新たな年を迎える神聖な夜です。

2 Buddhist temples ring the bells 108 times around the midnight of the New Year's Eve. While the bell is ringing, people eat *toshikoshi soba*.

訳 仏教の寺は大晦日の深夜前後に108回鐘を鳴らします。鐘が鳴る間には年越しそばを食べます。

Toshikoshi means seeing the old year out and *soba* means noodles. People eat noodles, because their thin and long shape symbolizes a good long life.

訳 年越しとは古い一年を見送ること、蕎麦は麺のことです。麺を食べるのはその細く長い形が長生きを象徴するからです。

- □ customary
  形 習慣的な

- □ New Year's Eve
  大晦日
- □ sacred　形 神聖な
- □ let go of
  ～を手放す
- □ embrace　動 受け入れる

- □ ring　動 鳴らす

- □ see out　見送る
- □ symbolize
  動 象徴する

183

メニュー 69 新年のご馳走
New Year Feast

photo：june. / PIXTA（ピクスタ）

photo：熊鈴 / PIXTA（ピクスタ）

photo：june. / PIXTA（ピクスタ）

1 For the first three days of the year, people eat *osechi ryori*. A variety of foods are beautifully packed in special lacquer boxes called *jubako*. Since all foods are already prepared, everyone can relax and celebrate the New Year without the hustle of cooking.

☐ lacquer boxes
漆塗りの重箱
☐ hustle
動 〜を詰め込む

訳 新年の三が日にはおせち料理を食べます。多彩な料理が漆塗りの重箱という特別な箱に美しく詰められています。全ての料理がすでに調理済みなので、料理をする面倒なく皆リラックスして新年を祝うことができます。

2 Each item in the boxes has a wish. For example, shrimp is for a long life because the bent back and long beard resemble an old man. Black soybeans, or *kuromame*, are for hardworking, since *mame* means being diligent.

☐ bent　形 曲がった
☐ resemble
動 〜に似ている
☐ diligent　形 勤勉な

訳 重箱に入ったそれぞれの料理に願いが込められています。たとえば背が曲がり長いひげのあるエビは高齢の男性に煮ているため長生きのためです。黒豆は、「マメ」が勤勉を意味するため精励のためです。

3 Other New Year feasts include *ozoni*. It is a soup made with *mochi* rice cake. *Zo* means miscellaneous and the recipes differ among regions. *Otoso* is spiced *sake*, which is served with *osechi* for good health.

☐ feast　名 ご馳走
☐ miscellaneous
形 雑多な
☐ spiced
形 薬草の入った

訳 その他の新年のご馳走にお雑煮があります。餅を入れた汁物のことです。「雑」とは様々なものを意味し、レシピは地方によって異なります。お屠蘇は健康を願っておせちとともに出される、薬草を入れたお酒です。

行事食
Festive Fare

メニュー 70 子供のための祝いの食べ物
Children's Fare

photo：Hunny / PIXTA（ピクスタ）

photo：june

photo：Chi− / PIXTA（ピクスタ）

説明してみよう！

1 There are special holidays for children in Japan. March 3rd is *hinamatsuri* (the doll festival) or Girl's Day. It is the day to pray girl's health and happiness. Colorful rice crackers, *chirashi zushi* (*sushi* rice topped with a variety of fish and vegetables) and *amazake* (sweet non-alcoholic *sake*) are enjoyed at *hinamatsuri*.

□pray 動 祈る
□rice cracker あられ

訳▶日本には子供のための祝日があります。3月3日はひな祭りで、女の子の日とも言います。女の子の健康と幸せを祈る日です。色とりどりのあられ、ちらし寿司（様々な魚介や野菜をのせた鮨米）、甘酒（甘いアルコールなしのお酒）を楽しみます。

2 May 5th is *tango no sekku*, or Boy's Day. It is celebrated for boy's health and advancement. *Kashiwa mochi* is served on this day. It is *mochi* filled with sweet *adzuki* beans and wrapped with an oak leaf.

□advancement 名 出世
□oak leaf 名 柏の葉

訳▶5月5日は端午の節句、男の子の日です。男の子の健康と出世を願う日です。端午の節句では柏餅が出されます。これは甘いあずき豆を詰め柏の葉で巻いたものです。

3 *Shichi go san* is celebrated on November 15th. Boys at 3 and 5, girls at 3 and 7 years old dress up and visit shrines for healthy growth. The children get *chitose ame* (thousand year candy), which is a long thin red and white candy. The length symbolizes longevity and the colors represent good luck.

□shrine 名 神社
□longevity 名 長寿

訳▶11月15日は七五三です。男の子は3歳と5歳、女の子は3歳と7歳で、健康を願い着飾って神社を訪れます。子供達は千歳飴という紅白の長い飴をもらいます。その長さは長寿、色は幸運を表しています。

洋食
Yoshoku

洋食は単なる西洋料理にとどまらず、多くの日本人にとって郷愁的な響きをもつ独自の料理文化です。代表的な洋食の魅力を紹介しましょう。

洋食—Facts

- 日本初の洋食レストラン開業の年 (he year of first *yoshoku* restaurant founded)—1863年
- 元祖三大洋食 (the original 3 best *yoshoku*)—
  トンカツ (*tonkatsu*), コロッケ (*korokke*), カレー (curry)

① Japanese-style western food
和風の西洋料理

 85

Yoshoku means western cuisine as opposed to *washoku*. But it also means uniquely developed Japanese-style western dishes. Many western-style dishes were introduced to Japan in the Meiji period. Some of the recipes were modified and they have become favorites of Japanese people.

□uniquely 副 独自に
□modify 動 手を加える

 洋食とは和食に対する西洋料理のことです。しかし独自に発展した和風の西欧料理も意味します。多くの西欧料理が明治時代に日本に入ってきました。その内のいくつかのレシピに手が加えられ、日本人の大好物になりました。

The classic *yoshoku* dishes include curry rice, *ebi* fry (fried shrimp), and *korokke* (croquette made with potatoes and meat).

□croquette 名 コロッケ

訳 代表的な洋食料理には、カレーライス、エビフライ (エビの揚げ物)、コロッケ (ポテトと肉のコロッケ) などがあります。

② The charm of nostalgia
郷愁の魅力

Yoshoku has a special appeal of nostalgia to the Japanese. It is an icon of the *Showa* period, and the never-changing tastes of the classic dishes bring back people's memories. A great place to feel the nostalgia is authentic *yoshoku* restaurants called *yoshoku ya*.

□nostalgia 名 郷愁
□icon 名 象徴
□authentic
形 本物の

訳 日本人にとって洋食には特別な郷愁の魅力があります。洋食は昭和時代の象徴であり、古典的な料理の変わらぬ味は、過去の記憶を呼び戻します。その郷愁を感じるには、洋食屋と呼ばれる本格洋食料理店がいいでしょう。

③ Popular at *famiresu*
ファミレスで人気

You can eat *yoshoku* dishes in other places too. *Famiresu* ("Family restaurants") are casual and inexpensive chain restaurants. *Okosama* lunch is a popular item at *famiresu*. It is a plate of selected *yoshoku* dishes specially made for children. Some of the Japanese-style cafés called *kissaten* serve *yoshoku* dishes too.

□inexpensive
形 安価な

訳 洋食料理はその他の場所でも食べることができます。ファミレス（ファミリーレストラン）はカジュアルで手頃なチェーン店。お子様ランチはファミレスで人気の商品です。子供用に洋食各品を一皿に盛ったものです。また喫茶店という和風のカフェでも洋食を出すところがあります。

その他人気の洋食には、ハヤシライス(beef stew with a demi-glace sauce)、ドリア(rice casserole with a white sauce)などがあります！

洋食
Yoshoku

175kcal　￥〜1,500

メニュー
73

オムライス
Omu rice / Omelet and Rice

photo：スミスジョージ / PIXTA（ピクスタ）

料理のキーワード

 egg（卵）, rice（米）, onion（玉ねぎ）, ketchup（ケチャップ）,
butter（バター）, chicken stock（鶏ガラスープ）,
demi-glacé sauce（デミグラスソース）, béchamel sauce
（ベシャメルソース）

 wrap in（包む）, shape into（〜の形にする）, plate（盛り付け
る）, top with（〜をかける）

190

説明してみよう！

86

1 *Omu* rice means "omelet and rice". Flavored rice is wrapped in a thin sheet of omelet. It is shaped into an oval. Making a thin yet solid sheet of eggs is challenging for cooks. The rice is flavored with ingredients, such as chicken stock, onion, ketchup and butter. The sweetness of ketchup and onion complement the flavor of chicken.

□shape into
　形作る
□oval　形 楕円形の
□solid
　形 しっかりした
□complement
　動 補足する

訳 オムライスは「オムレツとライス」の意味です。味をつけたライスをオムレツで包んだものです。楕円形になっています。薄くしかもしっかりとした卵焼きを作るのは容易ではありません。ライスは鶏のだし、玉ねぎ、ケチャップ、バターなどの食材で味をつけてあります。

Omu rice is also topped with ketchup. Cutting into the just-plated *omu* rice, you will enjoy the aroma coming out of the warm flavored rice inside.

□come out of
　〜から出てくる

訳 オムライスにはケチャップがかかっています。皿に盛ったばかりのオムライスにナイフを入れると、中の温かい味付きライスから立ち上る、豊かな風味を楽しめます。

2 There are variations of *omu* rice. The topping can be demi-glace sauce or béchamel sauce instead of ketchup. *Omu* curry is omu rice plated together with Japanese curry. *Omu soba* is noodles wrapped in a sheet of omelet instead of rice.

□béchamel sauce
　ベシャメル (ホワイト)
　ソース
□plate　動 盛り付ける

訳 オムライスにはバリエーションがあります。トッピングはケチャップの代わりにデミグラソースはベシャメルソースが使われることもあります。オムカレーは、和風カレーと一緒に皿に盛ったオムライスです。オムそばは、米の代わりに麺をオムレツで包んだものです。

220kcal　¥〜1,500

メニュー 74

ハンバーグ

Hambagu / Japanese-style Hambagu steak

photo：ささざわ / PIXTA (ピクスタ)

料理のキーワード

 食材

ground beef（牛のひき肉）/ blend of beef and pork（合い挽き肉）, onion（玉ねぎ）, egg（卵）, breadcrumbs（パン粉）, milk（牛乳）, ketchup（ケチャップ）, oyster sauce（オイスターソース）, Worcestershire sauce（ウスターソース）, *daikon* radish（大根）, mushroom（マッシュルーム）, cheese（チーズ）, sunny-side egg（目玉焼き）

 調理法

knead（生地をこねる）, hand-shape（手で形作る）, fry（焼く）

😊 **味わい**

demi-glacé（デミグラス）, teriyaki（てりやき）

説明してみよう!

⬇87

1 *Hambagu* is a steak of a round or oval-shaped patty made with ground beef, onions, eggs and breadcrumbs. The meat may be a blend of beef and pork.

訳 ハンバーグは、ひき肉、玉ねぎ、卵とパン粉で作った円形もしくは楕円形のパティのステーキです。肉は牛と豚の合挽きである場合もあります。

The name *hambagu* is said to have come from the dish made in the German city of Hamburg in 18th century. The original dish was brought to the US by German immigrants and became Hamburg steak. The Japanese eventually adopted it to their diet.

訳 ハンバーグの名はドイツの都市ハンブルグで18世紀に作られた料理に由来すると言われます。起源となる料理はドイツ移民からアメリカにもたらされ、ハンバーグステーキになりました。日本人がやがてそれを食生活に取り入れます。

2 There are a variety of sauces for *hambagu*. A blend of ketchup, oyster sauce and Worcestershire sauce is common. Other popular sauces include soy sauce and grated *daikon*, demi-glace and teriyaki. *Hambagu* may be topped with mushrooms, cheese, or a sunny-side egg. It is often served with rice or spaghetti.

訳 ハンバーグには多彩なソースがあります。ケチャップ、オイスターソースとウスターソースのブレンドは一般的です。他の人気のソースには、醤油と大根おろし、デミグラ、照り焼きなどがあります。ハンバーグはキノコ、チーズ、目玉焼きがトッピングになることもあります。よくライスやスパゲッティが添えられています。

□ round 形 円形の
□ patty 名 パテ
□ ground 挽いた
□ breadcrumbs 名 パン粉

□ adopt to ～へ取り入れる

□ Worcestershire sauce ウスターソース
□ grated 形 すりおろした

洋食
Yoshoku

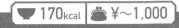
170kcal | ¥～1,000

メニュー
75

ナポリタン
Naporitan / Spaghetti with Ketchup Sauce

photo：assy / PIXTA (ピクスタ)

料理のキーワード

 食材　spaghetti (スパゲティ), ketchup (ケチャップ), onion (玉ねぎ), green pepper (ピーマン), mushroom (マッシュルーム), ham (ハム)/ bacon (ベーコン)/sausage (ソーセージ), Parmesan cheese (パルメザンチーズ)

 調理法　boil (茹でる), stir-fry (炒める)

 味わい　soft (柔らかい), al dente (アルデンテ), concentrated sweetness (凝縮された甘味)

説明してみよう！

⬇88

1 *Naporitan* is a classic *yoshoku* dish made with spaghetti and a ketchup-based sauce. The sauce is typically is made with ketchup, onion, green pepper and mushrooms. Julienned ham, bacon or sausage is also added to the sauce.

□green pepper
ピーマン
□julienne
動 細切りする

訳 ナポリタンは、スパゲッティとケチャップ系ソースで作る代表的な洋食料理です。ソースは通常ケチャップ、玉ねぎ、ピーマンとキノコで作ります。細切りにしたはむ、ベーコンかソーセージもソースに加えます。

It is normally served with grated parmesan cheese. The texture of the noodles is originally soft, but you can find firmer "al dente" nowadays.

訳 普通おろしたパルメザンチーズが付いてきます。麺の食感は本来やわらかいものですが、最近ではより固い「アルデンテ」のものもあります。

2 They say that a chef in Yokohama invented the dish after World War II. He saw American soldiers eat spaghetti flavored with ketchup instead of tomato sauce. Since tomatoes were not easily available back then, the dish became popular among eateries in town. The chef improved the taste by using fresh tomatoes and the legendary dish was born.

□invention 名 考案
□back then
その当時

訳 第二次世界大戦後に、横浜のシェフがこの料理を発案したと言われます。そのシェフは米軍兵士がトマトソースの代わりにケチャップで味付けしたスパゲティを食べるのを見ます。当時トマトは容易には入手できず、この料理は街の飲食店でも人気になりました。シェフは新鮮なトマトを使って味を改良し、この伝統的な料理が生まれました。

喫茶店文化
The *Kissaten* Culture

喫茶店は単にティーやコーヒーショップを意味します。しかし日本の喫茶店文化はとてもユニークです。まず、迅速なサービスを主眼に置いた欧米のコーヒーチェーンとは異なり、喫茶店はゆっくりくつろぎ、静かに飲み物を楽しむ場所です。二番目に、一つひとつ淹れる質の高い飲み物を提供します。三つ目に、バター付きの日本の柔らかいトースト、フルーツと生クリームを挟んだふわふわのサンドイッチほか、喫茶店はクラシックな洋食を食べることができる場所です。

喫茶店は日本各地にありますが、ことに名古屋では人々の生活の大きな一部です。喫茶店が数多く存在するため、中には競争に勝つべく、朝の営業時間中にコーヒー一杯で無料の朝食を出す店もあります。

Kissaten simply means a tea or coffee shop. But the Japanese *kissaten* culture is very unique. First, unlike other western-style coffee chains that focus on a speedy service, *kissaten* is a place to slow down and enjoy a cup of drink in a quiet setting. Second, they serve high-quality drinks that are individually prepared. Third, you can find classic *yoshoku* dishes at *kissaten*, such as a buttered toast of Japanese-style soft bread and fluffy sandwiches filled with fruits and fresh cream.

There are classic *kissaten* all over Japan, but it is a big part of the life of people particularly in Nagoya. There are so many of them that some *kissaten* serve free breakfast for a cup of coffee during the morning service hours to win the competition.

ご当地料理

Regional Cuisine

ご当地料理
Regional Cuisine

伝統的な郷土料理と地域復興の願いから近年新たに生みだされたご当地料理。どちらも多彩な日本の食文化を象徴しています。

ご当地料理─Facts

photo：kuro3 / PIXTA（ピクスタ）

- 郷土料理の数（the number of traditional regional dishes）─2,126（品）
- 人気の郷土料理（the most popular regional dishes）─
  ①いも煮（*imoni*）　②鶏飯（*keihan*）　③きりたんぽ（*kiritanpo*）

参照：文化庁「平成28年度伝統的な生活文化実態調査事業報告書【郷土食】」

① The diversity of regional *washoku*
和食の地方料理の多様性　⬇89

Japan consists of five main islands. From north to south, these are Hokkaido, Honshu, Shikoku, Kyushu and Okinawa. The islands are divided into eight regions. These are Hokkaido, Tohoku, Kanto, Chubu, Kinki, Chugoku, Shikoku and Kyushu.

 日本は五つの主な島から成っています。北から南に北海道、本州、四国、九州、沖縄です。これらの島は八つの地方に分けられます。北海道、東北、関東、中部、近畿、中国、四国、九州です。

In addition, there are 47 prefectures. Because of the microclimate of each prefecture you can find a wide array of unique dishes that feature local ingredients throughout Japan.

 さらに日本には47の都道府県があります。各県でより細かな気候が存在するため、多彩で個性的な料理を全国で見つけることができます。

□consist of
　〜から構成される
□divided into
　〜に分けられる

□microclimate
　名 細かい気候

198

② *Kyodo ryori* and *gotochi ryori*
郷土料理とご当地料理

Traditional regional dishes are called *kyodo ryori*. They have been enjoyed by the locals for centuries and become a part of the culture of the area. Also, there are newer dishes that have been developed to create regional attractions. These are called *gotochi ryori*. *Gyoza* dumplings in Tochigi Prefecture and Kobe beefsteak in Hyogo Prefecture are good examples.

□attraction 名 魅力
□dumpling 名 団子

訳 伝統的な地方料理を郷土料理と言います。何世紀にも渡りその土地の人々に楽しまれ、地元文化の一部となったものです。地域の呼び物作りとして生まれた新たな料理もあります。これらはご当地料理と呼ばれます。栃木県の餃子、兵庫県の神戸牛ステーキなどが好例です。

③ Regional variations
地域によるバリエーション

There may be regional variations of the same dish. For example, what is known as *sushi* globally is the Tokyo-style *nigiri*. *Sushi* can be giant rolls filled with a variety of ingredients in Chiba. *Sushi* is fermented in the ancient style in Shiga, and wrapped in bamboo leaves in Nagano. It is a bowl with a variety of fish and vegetables in Okayama.

□giant 形 巨大な
□ferment
　動 発酵する

訳 地方によりバリエーションがある料理も存在します。例えば世界で鮨として知られているのは東京流の握りです。千葉では多彩な具材を詰めた巻物です。滋賀では古代の手法で発酵させてありますし、長野ではササの葉に包まれています。岡山では様々な魚や野菜の丼です。

199

北海道・東北
Hokkaido & Tohoku

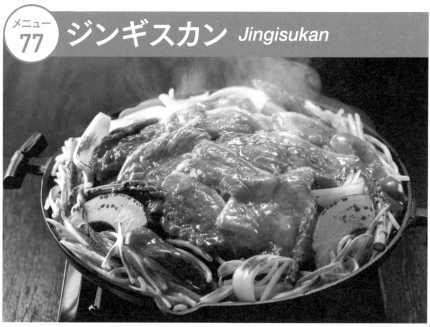

メニュー 77 ジンギスカン *Jingisukan*

羊のバーベキュー Lamb Barbecue

You rarely find lamb dishes in Japan.
Jingisukan is a barbecue of lamb or mutton.
The meat is flavored with ingredients such as soy sauce, sugar, grated apples, ginger and garlic.

訳 日本で子羊の料理を目にするのは稀です。ジンギスカンは子羊または成熟羊のバーベキューです。肉は醤油、砂糖、おろしリンゴ、生姜、ニンニクなどで味をつけます。

It is cooked with vegetables in a special iron pot called *Jingisukan nabe*. The bottom of the pot is convex to drain off the fat from the meat.

訳 野菜と一緒にジンギスカン鍋という特殊な鉄鍋で調理します。この鍋底は肉の脂を切るため凸型になっています。

□ barbecue
　名 バーベキュー
□ lamb　名 子羊
□ mutton　名 成熟羊
□ grated
　動 すりおろした

□ convex　形 凸状の
□ drain off　〜を切る

200

日本の最北部であり最大の農産地である北海道、そして本州北東部に位置し六つの県からなる東北地方では、冬の寒さをしのぐ多くの料理が生み出されました。

メニュー 78 きりたんぽ *Kiritanpo*

photo：たけちゃん / PIXTA（ピクスタ）

ご飯の焼き団子 Grilled Rice Dumplings

Kiritanpo is a cylinder-shaped rice dumpling from Akita Prefecture. Mashed rice is spread on a wooden skewer and grilled over an open hearth. It is eaten with *miso*.

 きりたんぽは秋田産の、円筒形の米の団子です。つぶした米を木の棒に塗りつけ炉端で焼きます。味噌をつけて食べます。

It is also an ingredient of the hotpot called *kiritanpo nabe*. The rice is removed from the stick and cooked in a pot with chicken and vegetables.

訳 きりたんぽ鍋の素材にもなります。米は棒から外し、鍋に入れて鶏肉と野菜とともに煮ます。

□ **cylinder** 名 円筒
□ **mash** 動 つぶす
□ **spread on** ～に塗る
□ **skewer** 名 串
□ **open hearth** 炉端
□ **stick** 名 棒

メニュー 79 ちゃんこ鍋 *Chanko Nabe*

photo：june. / PIXTA (ピクスタ)

相撲力士の好物 *Sumo* Wrestlers' Favorite

Chanko nabe is a hotpot that is known as an important dish to nourish *sumo* wrestlers. There is no specific recipe for *chanko nabe*. The junior wrestlers prepare it for the entire team.

> **訳** ちゃんこ鍋は相撲力士の栄養摂取に重要な料理として知られ
> ます。ちゃんこ鍋に特定のレシピはありません。下の級の力
> 士が部屋全員用に作ります。

☐nourish
動 栄養を摂る
☐entire 形 全体の

You can find *chanko nabe* restaurants run by former *sumo* wrestlers, in particular in Ryogoku, Tokyo. It is the home of the *Kokugikan sumo* stadium.

> **訳** ことに東京の両国では、元力士が経営するちゃんこ鍋店が見
> つかります。この地域には相撲のスタジアム、国技館がある
> のです。

☐run 動 経営する

関東は東京と他6つの県からなる、都市圏と肥沃な農産地帯のどちらももつ地域です。世界有数のミシュラン星付きレストランが多数ある反面、素朴な地元料理も豊富に存在します。

メニュー 80 サザエのつぼ焼き Grilled Turban Shell

photo：撮るねっと / PIXTA（ピクスタ）

潮の香り The Scent Of The Sea

Sazae (turban shell) is one of the most prized shellfish in Japan. Kanagawa Prefecture is one of the most famous regions for the grilled *sazae* dish. The spiral meat of the shellfish is grilled in its large shell and served hot. It releases the flavor of the sea at the table.

訳 サザエは日本で珍重される貝の一つです。神奈川県は焼いたサザエの料理で知られる地域の一つです。渦を巻いた貝の身は、その大きな殻の中で焼かれて熱々で出されます。潮の香りを食卓に放ちます。

□ **turban shell**
サザエ

□ **prized**
形 珍重される

□ **spiral**
形 らせん状の

□ **release**
動 〜を放つ

203

メニュー81 朴葉味噌 *Hoba Miso*

photo：ささざわ / PIXTA（ピクスタ）

味噌と棒葉の味わい Flavors of Miso and Magnolia Leaf

Hoba miso is a dish from the beautiful mountain region Hida-Takayama in Gifu Prefecture. Mountain vegetables such as mushrooms and other vegetables are dressed with *miso* and placed on the dried magnolia leaf.

訳▶朴葉味噌は岐阜県飛騨高山の美しい山岳地帯の料理です。キノコなどの山菜と他の素材に味噌をからめ、乾燥させた朴葉にのせます。

□ mountain
  vegetables　山菜
□ magnolia leaf
  朴葉

After baked over a charcoal grill, the aroma of the leaf imparts to the ingredients. They are eaten with hot rice.

訳▶炭火で焼くと葉の風味が食材に移ります。熱いご飯とともに食べます。

□ charcoal grill
  炭火焼き
□ impart
  動 分け与える

204

中部は日本海や太平洋に接する県、山岳地帯の県と様々な地理にあります。そのため優れた日本酒が有名な雪の多い長野、日中は暖かく夜は寒いことからワインの名産地である山梨など多様な食文化がみられます。

メニュー 82 治部煮 *Jibuni*

photo：ami / PIXTA (ピクスタ)

鴨肉／鶏肉の煮込み Simmered Duck/Chicken

The city of Kanazawa thrived during the Edo period and created a rich food culture. *Jibuni* is a specialty of the city. Sliced duck or chicken is dusted with flour and simmered in a soy sauce-based broth. The flour seals the *umami* of the meat. It is served with vegetables, *fu* (flour cake) and *wasabi*.

□thrive 動 繁栄する
□dusted with 〜をまぶす
□broth 名 だし
□seal 動 封じ込める
□cake 名 かたまり

訳 金沢市は江戸時代に繁栄し、豊かな食文化を生み出しました。治部煮はこの街の名物です。鴨か鶏の薄切りに小麦粉をまぶし、醤油系のだし汁で煮ます。小麦粉が肉の旨味を閉じ込めます。野菜、麩(小麦を固めたもの)とわさびとともに出されます。

メニュー 83 ゆうべし *Yubeshi*

photo：十津川村役場

柚子の詰め物 Stuffed *Yuzu* Citrus

Yubeshi is a preserved food made by stuffing *yuzu* dish from Totsukawamura village, Nara Prefecture. The cored *yuzu* citrus is filled with ingredients such as *miso*, sesame seeds, buchwheat flour and bonito flakes. It is then steamed and hung outside to dry and age for a few months. It is enjoyed with sake or as a side dish.

訳 ゆうべしは奈良県十津川村の柚子に詰め物をした保存食です。中身をくり抜いた柚子に味噌、ごま、そば粉、かつお節などの素材を詰めます。そして蒸し、乾燥熟成させるために数ヶ月外に吊るします。酒のつまみや副菜として楽しみます。

□cored 形 くりぬいた
□citrus 名 柑橘類
□bonito flakes
　　かつお節
□hang 動 吊るす
□age 動 熟成させる

206

近畿は本州中西部の7つの府県をもつ地域です。京都には、京料理と呼ばれる貴族、寺院らに作りあげられた独自の料理があります。大阪には庶民が生んだ多彩な料理が、他地域では和牛、原産フルーツや野菜などが知られます。

メニュー 84 京漬物 Kyoto-style pickles

photo：kuro3 / PIXTA（ピクスタ）

京野菜の漬物 *Kyo Yasai* Pickles

Kyo Yasai means vegetables native to Kyoto. They have unique shapes, colors and flavors. They are often made into pickles. For example, pickled *Shogoin* turnip is classic. The turnip is juicy and sweet with a smooth texture. The pickles are made in the very thinly sliced *senmaizuke*-style ("1,000 slice in a barrel") and flavored with vinegar, *kombu*, sugar and chili pepper.

□ **native** 形 原産の
□ **turnip** 名 カブ
□ **barrel** 名 樽

訳▶ 京野菜とは京都原産野菜のことです。ユニークな形や色、風味を持っています。これらはよく漬物にします。例えば聖護院かぶの漬物は代表的です。このかぶは汁気が多く甘味があり、なめらかな食感を持ちます。漬物はとても薄く切った千枚漬け（「ひと樽に千枚入っている」の意）で、酢、昆布、砂糖と唐辛子で味をつけます。

四国・中国
Shikoku & Chugoku

当地料理

⬇94

メニュー 85 お好み焼き *Okonomiyaki*

photo：ささざわ / PIXTA（ピクスタ）

料理系パンケーキ Savory Pancake

Okonomiyaki is a savory pancake cooked on a large hotplate. *Okonomi* means "as you like" and the recipes differ depending on the region. The popular Osaka style is made with flour and various ingredients such as shredded cabbage, seafood and meat. It is flavored with a special sauce, mayonnaise and seaweed flakes.
The Hiroshima-style is unique because it also contains noodles and is shaped like a sandwich.

- □ savory 形 料理系の
- □ depending on ～による
- □ shredded 千切りした
- □ seaweed flakes 青海苔
- □ contain 動 含む

訳 お好み焼きは大きな鉄板で焼く料理系のパンケーキです。お好みとは「好きなように」という意味で、地域によりレシピは異なります。人気の高い大阪風は小麦粉に、刻みキャベツ、魚介や肉など様々な具材で作ります。特製ソース、マヨネーズ、青海苔などで味をつけます。広島風は麺を含んでサンドイッチ状になっており、独自性があります。

208

中国地方は日本海に面し、四国は太平洋と内海である瀬戸内海の間にあります。どちらも本州の南に位置します。この地域は みかん、なし、もも、ぶどうなどの果物を含む様々な食材で知られます。

メニュー 86 フグ Blowfish

photo:ひろゆき / PIXTA (ピクスタ)

毒なしの珍味 Poison-free Delicacy

Blowfish, or *fugu*, is known for being poisonous. But it is safe to eat it in Japan, because it is cooked only by licensed professionals. Yamaguchi Prefecture is famous for *fugu* dishes. For example, *sashimi* is so thinly sliced that you can see the beautiful prints of the plate through the flesh.

- □ blowfish 名 フグ
- □ poisonous 形 有毒な
- □ licensed 形 免許を持った
- □ print 名 模様
- □ flesh 名 肉

訳 フグは毒があることで知られます。しかし日本では免許を持ったプロだけが調理をするので安全です。山口県はフグ料理で知られます。たとえば刺身はとても薄く切ってあるので、美しい皿の模様を魚の身を通して見ることができます。

メニュー 87 ちゃんぽん *Chanpon*

photo:しまじろう / PIXTA (ピクスタ)

「色々入った」麺入りスープ "A Mix Of Many Things" Noodle Soup

Chanpon is a noodle soup from Nagasaki. *Chanpon* means "a mix of many". Various ingredients such as pork, fish cake, bean sprouts, cabbage and carrots are stir-fried. They are put into a bowl of *dashi* stock and milk, along with chewy Chinese-style noodles. It is popular for the deep, rich creamy flavor.

□**many** 代 多くのもの
□**fish cake** かまぼこ
□**bean sprout** もやし
□**stir-fried** 形 炒めた

訳 ちゃんぽんは長崎の麺入りスープです。ちゃんぽんは「色々混ぜたもの」を意味します。豚、かまぼこ、もやし、キャベツ、ニンジンほか多彩な具材を炒めます。それらを出汁と牛乳、コシの強い中華麺の入ったどんぶりに入れます。深みのある濃厚でクリーミーな味で人気があります。

210

日本の南西部の九州島と沖縄諸島からなる九州・沖縄。九州島の火山質の土はさつまいもを育てるのにぴったりで、芋焼酎で有名です。沖縄は中国やアジア、アメリカなどの文化を取り入れた独自の料理を誇ります。

メニュー 88 ミミガー *Mimiga*

photo：USSIE / PIXTA（ピクスタ）

サステイナブルな食生活：豚の耳 Sustainable Diet: Pork Ears

Pork is eaten in Okinawa literally from head to tail. For example, *mimiga* is a steamed or boiled pig's ear. It may sound weird, but it has a nice crunchiness. Also, it is rich in collagen. *Mimiga* is typically served with a soy sauce and vinegar, or a creamy peanut sauce.

訳 沖縄で豚を文字通り頭から尻尾まで食べます。例えばミミガーは、蒸すもしくは茹でた豚の耳です。おかしなものに聞こえるかもしれませんが、歯ごたえのいいコリッとした食感があります。またコラーゲンも豊富です。ミミガーは通常醤油と酢、もしくはクリーミーなピーナツバターのソースと一緒に食べます。

☐ literally
副 文字通り

☐ weird 形 奇妙な

☐ crunchiness
名 コリコリした食感

☐ collagen
名 コラーゲン

精進料理

Shojin Ryori

植物系の食べ物が最近各国で人気を集めています。肉や魚介なしに野菜と穀物のみで作られているため、精進料理はベジタリアンやヴィーガンには理想的です。精進料理は命を殺めることを罪とする仏教の教えに基づいています。これは 14 世紀に日本にもたらされた料理です。

精進料理は専門の料理店や幾つかの仏教のお寺で見つかります。動物性タンパク質なしで、料理各品は驚くほど風味豊かで栄養価に富んでいます。例えば胡麻豆腐はおろしたごまと日本特有の葛というデンプンを合わせて固めたものです。けんちん汁は根菜と豆腐で作る透明なスープです。スープは昆布をベースにした出汁で作ります。風呂吹き大根は厚く切った大根を煮て甘い味噌のソースをのせたたものです。

Plant-based foods are becoming popular nowadays in many countries. *Shojin ryori* is ideal for vegetarians and vegans, because it is made only with vegetables and grains without meat or seafood. *Shojin ryori* is based on a principle of Buddhism that it is a sin to take life. It was brought to Japan in 14th century.

You can find *shojin ryori* dishes at specialized restaurants and some Buddhist temples. They are surprisingly flavorful and nutritious without animal protein. For example, *goma-dofu* is a cake made with ground sesame seeds and a unique Japanese root vegetable starch *kudzu*. *Kenchinjiru* is a clear soup of root vegetables and *tofu*. The soup is made with *kombu*-based *dashi* stock. *Furofuki daikon* is a simmered thickly-cut *daikon* radish topped with a sweet miso sauce.

コンビニ

konbini

・・

日本には5万軒以上のコンビニが存在します。これらは他国のコンビニとはとても異なります。例えば米国ではよくガソリンスタンドに隣接し、必要最低限の商品を販売します。しかし日本のコンビニは食べ物、アルコール、本から日用雑貨まで置いています。またコンビニで公共料金の支払い、コンサートチケットの購入、清潔なトイレの使用まで可能です。多くの店では無料wifiもあります。言葉を変えれば、多くの日本人にとってコンビニは生活の一部なのです。

コンビニの食べ物は包装入りのスナックや飲料の域をはるかに超えています。温かいお弁当、和風のサンドイッチやパン類、和菓子、コーヒー、ビール、日本酒からウイスキーまで見つかります。コンビニは、様々な美味しい食べ物を手頃な値段で買うのにとてもいい場所です。

There are over 50,000 convenience stores (*konbini*) in Japan. They are very different from those in other countries. For example in the US, convenience stores are often located next to gas stations and sell only minimum items. But Japanese convenience stores offer everything from food, alcohol, books to drugstore items. Also, you can pay your utility bills, buy concert tickets and use their clean bathrooms. Many of them have free wifi too. In other words, *konbini* is a part of life for many Japanese people. Food at *konbini* is far beyond packaged snacks and drinks. You can find hot bento boxes, *onigiri*, Japanese-style sandwiches and pastries, *wagashi*, coffee, beer, sake and whisky. *konbini* is a great place to buy many types of delicious food at reasonable prices.

●著者紹介

片山晶子 Akiko Katayama

ニューヨーク在住ジャーナリスト。飲食業界に関するトピックを広くカバーする。英語版 Forbes.com コラムニスト。100万人の聴衆を持つニューヨークのラジオ局「ヘリテージ・レディオ・ネットワーク」で和食文化を世界に伝える番組「JAPAN EATS!」のホスト兼プロデューサーを務め世界190カ国に聴衆を持つ。「ヘリテージ・レディオ・ネットワーク」役員。和食への理解促進を目的とする米国非営利団体「New York Japanese Culinary Academy」理事。日本政府・民間企業に対する日米飲食ビジネス関連コンサルティングや調査、伝統食品生産者の対米進出の支援活動にも従事している。米国版「料理の鉄人」"Iron Chef America"、Netflix「ファイナル・テーブル」審査員。英国 London School of Economics & Political Science 修士課程、New York University Stern School of Business MBA 修了。ワイン＆スピリッツ国際認定資格 WSET 上級保有。

本書へのご意見・ご感想は下記URLまでお寄せください。
https://www.jresearch.co.jp/contact/

カバーデザイン・口絵デザイン	喜田里子
本文デザイン・DTP	株式会社シーツ・デザイン
本文イラスト	Tsuki
カバータイトル筆文字	竹内一
カバー写真（左から掲載順）	dronepc55 / photoAC ささざわ / PIXTA（ピクスタ）, Caito / PIXTA（ピクスタ）, jun / PIXTA（ピクスタ）

英語でガイド！
外国人がいちばん食べたい　和食90選

令和2年（2020年）　1月10日　初版第1刷発行
令和2年（2020年）　3月10日　第2刷発行

著　者　片山 晶子
発行人　福田 富与
発行所　有限会社 Jリサーチ出版
　　　　〒166-0002 東京都杉並区高円寺北2-29-14-705
　　　　電話 03（6808）8801（代）　FAX 03（5364）5310
　　　　編集部 03（6808）8806
　　　　https://www.jresearch.co.jp
印刷所　（株）シナノ パブリッシング プレス

ISBN978-4-86392-461-1 禁無断転載。なお、乱丁・落丁はお取り替えいたします。

音声ダウンロードのしかた

STEP1

インターネットで「https://audiobook.jp/exchange/ jresearch」にアクセス！

※上記の URL を入力いただくか、本ページ記載の QR コードを読み込んでください。

STEP2

表示されたページから、audiobook.jp への会員登録ページへ！

※音声のダウンロードには、オーディオブック配信サービス audiobook.jp への会員登録（無料）が必要です。すでに会員の方は STEP3 へお進みください。

STEP3

登録後、再度 STEP1 のページにアクセスし、シリアルコードの入力欄に「24611」を入力後、「送信」をクリック！

※作品がライブラリに追加されたと案内が出ます。

STEP4

必要な音声ファイルをダウンロード！

※スマートフォンやタブレットの場合は、アプリ「audiobook.jp」の案内が出ますので、アプリからご利用ください。

※ PC の場合は「ライブラリ」から音声ファイルをダウンロードしてご利用ください。

ご注意！

- PC からでも、iPhone や Android のスマートフォンやタブレットからでも音声を再生いただけます。
- 音声は何度でもダウンロード・再生いただくことができます。
- ダウンロード・アプリのご利用についてのお問い合わせ先：info@febe.jp （受付時間：平日 10 ～ 20 時）